Riding 500cc Two Strokes to Canada in 1972
And Other Motorcycle Adventures

Jim Balding and Jeffrey Ross

Dedicated to the Memory of
Larry Christopher Jr.
1953-2020

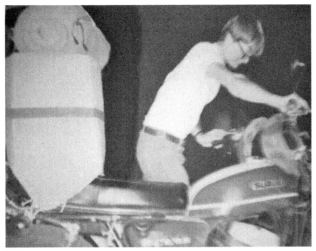

Larry and his Suzuki Titan June 1972

Other Motorcycle Adventure Stories:
Jim Balding
Terry Baugher
Ken Boltz
Jann M. Contento
Mike Newlun
Harry "Happy" Reynolds
Doyle Ross
Jeffrey Ross
Patricia Ross
Julie Sego

Jim and Jeff gratefully acknowledge assistance from Janine Balding and
Courtney Rene in terms of the overall content and production of this book.

Riding 500cc Two-Strokes from Arizona to Canada
By Jim Balding and Jeffrey Ross

Prelude: Jim

In June of 1972, Larry Christopher Jr., Jeff Ross, and I took a long motorcycle trip through the Midwest, West, and Canada. Jeff had just graduated from high school, and Larry and I weren't much older. Larry and I each had a 500cc Suzuki Titan, and Jeff piloted his 500cc Kawasaki Mach III triple. Jeff and I are going to describe that fun trip we took nearly a half century ago. But first, we thought you might like to learn a little about our history with motorcycles and our love of two-stroke engines. If you want to skip all the historical information, turn over to page eleven or thereabouts. Our Canada trip story begins there! Thanks.

Motorcycle Beginnings: Jim

I grew up in Stanfield, Arizona, about ten miles west of Casa Grande, Arizona, during the 1960s. My dad ran the cotton gin in Stanfield. I learned to ride in the desert and on backroads. My first machine was a homemade minibike. Dad and I made it out of electrical conduit and water pipes. We bent all the tubing ourselves to make the frame. The tires were from a go kart. We put some kind of sprockets on it and used an old 3 HP Briggs and Stratton engine. My minibike had almost straight gearing. I had to push it and jump on the minibike to get it going. Man, that was something. Those little minibikes had pretty much perpendicular forks—no rake or slant—so it was hairy hauling a** across the desert on that thing! There's an interesting back story to my minibike.

Back in the 1960s, one of my uncles had a 1/10 mile go kart racing track over in Ontario, California. Those karts used a Clinton two-stroke A490 motor—racing two-strokes which burned white gas and castor oil. They made 2 ½ horsepower at 7000 RPM. He also had a few karts with the much tamer Briggs & Stratton four-stroke motor. Some of his go karts had mounting plates for two of this Clinton engines. They would really haul! A couple of things happened to unfortunately put him out of business. One of his customers, a young girl, was pretty badly injured in a wreck, and her parents sued. Also, somebody bought the property next door and opened up a miniature golf course. They started complaining the howling two-stroke noise and the smell of burning oil was bothering customers. I guess he finally had enough. Eventually, my uncle sold out. We actually got two karts from him: one with the Briggs engine and one with the Clinton two-stroke. Dad and I put the Clinton two-stroke engine in my minibike, which would go about 60 mph with the Clinton engine and tall gearing!

As I became a little older, I acquired a nifty Honda 50 step-through. I was about 12-13 years old then. Later, I had a Honda 55. I horse-traded them both for a Suzuki Hillbilly 80.

A Suzuki Hillbilly

I remember going to the Suzuki shop on Apache Blvd in Mesa,

Arizona, off and on, to pick up parts. I rode that little bike for a few years. We'd change the gearing periodically for better hill climbing or dirt roads or whatever. I also had a Yamaha 80 Trailmaster. Eventually, I burned out a con rod bearing in the Hillbilly. I picked up the stuff to rebuild the engine, but I don't know if it ever really ran again. I eventually traded the Hillbilly 80 and the Yamaha to a guy who worked at the cotton gin for an interesting 1956 Chevy convertible, which had an Olds 394 V8 for a motor. The car had a push button starter with some issues, and the wiring under the hood and dash was burned up. I had to install a separate toggle switch to turn the ignition on and off. The ragtop was messed up, too, but I finally made the car presentable and running.

I had a Harley Hummer for a little while. Picked it up as a weird basket case: a six-volt electrical system 165cc two-stroke. Practically a rigid frame when I obtained it from the seller. The Hummer had some springer type forks for the front end. Crazy enough, the Hummer was also fitted with Goodyear Super Eagle tires, the kind which were sort of square on the bottom. I think the Hummer was some kind of restoration project which never got completed. And the bike didn't run. I remember gas was always dripping out of the worn-out Tillotson MT carburetor. No matter what I tried, I couldn't fix the worn-out carb.

But I managed to get the machine running and rideable. I had to be pretty creative. I used some felt gasket material to make homemade gaskets for the engine cases and an old aluminum bake pan to cut out a head gasket. I even used a standard paper handheld hole punch to make the holes in my homemade gaskets. I used some Copper Coat gasket sealant on the gaskets. When the original owner saw me riding the bike later, he didn't give me much credit. Apparently, he was kind of embarrassed since he couldn't get it to work.

I had a CL 175 Honda Scrambler for a time, too. The Honda was a SOHC (single overhead cam) four-stroke twin. I bought that motorcycle from another uncle of mine who had a feed and tack store in South Phoenix. He had taken the motorcycle in trade for some hay or feed. Couldn't have been worth too much. The bike didn't have any mufflers and was really loud. I rode the Honda back to Casa Grande the forty miles or so from Phoenix. I abused the Honda out in the desert frequently. The CL was always blowing fork seals and getting oil all over me. I spent a whole lot of time straightening out bent parts and pieces, like foot pegs and the gear shift lever, with a hammer. Our old Arizona desert was tough on motorcycles. D***, the Honda was obnoxiously loud!

Finally, I decided to buy a new bike. I used some of the money I received from the sale of a '56 Chevy I had fixed up to buy my new machine. I purchased a brand-new Suzuki X5 200cc scrambler. (The scrambler with the high pipes was actually called a TC 200.) The engine was kind of weak in the X5 models. I had to get the cylinders bored out numerous times, and I was always ordering parts for repairs. (To be fair, I have to reveal that I kept the engine at or over the tachometer redline most of the time. Might have been a significant contributing factor to my engine issues!)

I don't know how many times the Casa Grande cops pulled me over for speeding on my X5, like for doing 65 mph down Florence Boulevard where the posted speed was only 35 mph. But I never did get a ticket. I'd go zooming down the street past the Little Sombrero restaurant and get stopped by the police frequently—must have been five or six times. Nowadays, a guy would get arrested for felony speed or something and be cuffed and tossed into the squad car. Or a SWAT team would show up with traffic barricades. But they just told me to "slow it down." Didn't seem to stick.

I rode that Suzuki all over in the desert and crashed often. I went over the handlebars on several occasions and even had the bike run over me a time or two. The X5 was the bike I was riding when I first met Jeff. I got my 500 Titan, also new, in 1971.

A TC 200 Suzuki Scrambler
(Courtesy Suzuki Motors Corp)

I was able to buy my 500 Titan with money I earned working at the cotton gin for my dad. At the time, I was also a technology student at Central Arizona College in Coolidge, Arizona. Sometimes, after my evening classes at the college, I would work at the gin till midnight (at $1.85 an hour). I kept saving up money till I could buy a new $899 Suzuki T500.

Later, I kept the Titan and bought a Suzuki 750 Le Mans (a big water cooled two-stroke triple affectionately known as the Water Buffalo or Kettle) in 1973.

Jim's 1973 Suzuki 750 Le Mans

I finally sold my trusty old Titan to a fellow I worked with in the gin. He had ridden an X6 (a 250cc six-speed two-stroke Suzuki) earlier down to Honduras and crashed. He needed a replacement motorcycle. He rode my old Titan for a while. But then, one day, he had a jacket (supposedly securely strapped on) fall into the chain and bust up the countershaft sprocket. The incident did some other damage too. I don't know what eventually became of my old 500. Gone!

When I got to know Larry Christopher and Jeff Ross, I was riding the X5. Larry had a Yamaha Twin Jet 100. I actually met Larry on his first day of high school back in the late 60s. This occurred at good old Casa Grande Union High. We had US History class together. Larry and I also had study hall together. He was always drawing pictures of rockets and airplanes and showing them to me. He had a real fascination with cool mechanical things. Larry introduced me to Jeff a short time later. Jeff was a year or two younger than both of us. But he liked two-strokes, so we hit it off just fine. And we are still talking today.

While I had the Water Buffalo 750 in the early 80s, I picked up a 1979 Suzuki GS750 inline four four-stroke (gag). Bad mistake! The machine was faster but not nearly near as smooth or comfortable or quiet as the Water Buffalo. And I was bothered by the constant normal whine and clatter of the four-stroke engine, especially the cam chain and valve train noise. Anyway, I rode the GS750 for a couple years, then sold it.

I remember one Saturday, in 1983 or so, when Jeff and I took a seventy-five-mile ride from Casa Grande down to the pine-forested Mt. Lemmon near Tucson. I took my GS750, and he rode his 1982 GS550 Katana—a beautiful silver machine which was pretty fast for a two-valve head 550. BTW—on the way back, just as we were entering northern Tucson, I thought I'd cut through a service station to avoid stopping at a red light. Bad idea. I was awarded a ticket by TPD for "bypassing a traffic control device." @#$%!

Oh. Here's the funny back story to how I bought my four-stroke GS750. I spotted it for sale at the Harley Davidson dealership in Yuma, Arizona. (I was living nearby in Somerton and running the cotton gin at the time.) Seems a serviceman had traded it in for a Super Glide. Well, anyway, the salesman was very anxious to get rid of a Japanese bike which was contaminating his American-made showroom! He said it was stinking up the place. I got a sweet deal, but like I said earlier, I never really liked the four-stroke four-cylinder GS750 as much as my three-cylinder two-stroke Water Buffalo.

I later sold the 750 Water Buffalo to Larry. Of course, the time came when I longed for my old water pumper. But by then, production had ceased for the mighty street two-stokes. And my riding days were numbered.

I did own a Kawasaki Mach III for a little while. I bought that machine, and I believe it was a 1976 KH500 model, from our friend Rey Castellano, at a really good price—maybe $300 or $400. Rey was going through a tough spell at the time and needed some cash. He had a cool fiberglass road racing solo seat on the triple, and the motor was fitted with those K&N air filter pods. Rey's old bike was really fast and would wheelie no problem. But I never liked the way the Mach IIIs handled. Suzuki Titans have a long wheelbase and the center of gravity seems to be different than with the Mach III. The Titans are very road worthy and track well.

To me, those Kawasakis felt unstable in the front end above 100 mph, and the bike didn't feel right to me even at normal highway speeds. But like I said earlier, the 500 triple was fast. I eventually sold the Kawasaki to a kid who worked at our cotton gin. His mom, who worked in the front office at the gin, was mad at me for a long time for selling Rey's "Rocket" to him.

In 2011, I picked up a barn find 1976 GT500 Titan. The tired, sad machine had been sitting behind a welding shop, only partially covered under a lean-to, for about fifteen years, give or take a year.

Some clown had left the decrepit Titan out in the elements, pretty much to die a slow, excruciating death in the blistering Arizona sun. The disc-braked 500 only had 18,000 miles on the clock. The bike was in remarkably good shape except for sunbaked rubber components: the seat, tires, fork seals, brake hoses, and other erodible parts.

The old Titan's engine was free, and compression met near to new specs. A good fuel system flush, including the carbs, tank, and petcock, was needed badly. I changed the gear box oil and filled the oil injection tank. I initially mixed oil with gas in case it took a while for fresh oil to get through the injection lines. Well, three kicks and the engine came alive! After I did a little tinkering with the idle and mixture carburetor screws, that old machine ran great. No unwanted noises whatsoever. I decided to work on or replace the seat cover, handgrips, tires, tubes, fork seals, the chain, sprockets, the swing arm bushings, and I greased up the steering stem balls. I also put in a new master cylinder reservoir and installed new brake lines. The trial ride convinced me the old Titan was as nearly good as new. Success! I did a little buffing and polishing and touch-up on paint and chrome between rides. Eventually, I put a couple of thousand miles on the bike before selling it to a two-stroke collector from the Cave Creek, Arizona area in September 2019. This concludes my biking history (at least up till 2021). I still love bikes and being around them. There's something about the new Triumph Bonneville motorcycles and Royal Enfield 650s which is very fetching.

Jim's Restored GT-500 Titan

I also had some very interesting cars, most notably my 300 HP 1969 SS396 Camaro. But that's a different story. Incidentally, when I first got the Camaro, the motor was using oil at a high rate. I knew early Chevrolet big blocks were having valve guide issues. I had the valve guides knurled and installed new umbrella valve stem seals. No more oil issues. I drove my Camaro all around for a few years. But I finally got rid of it. For one thing, the car didn't have any A/C, and my bright orange Chevy had a black interior. The Arizona heat made cruising around Casa Grande tough in the summertime, even at night. Plus, I went through four or five clutches and several busted U-joints. Not to mention countless L60 X 14 tires. You might say I enjoyed keeping the big block Chevy at the redline, too. I sold it for around $1500. What a mistake. Nowadays, a company called Vintage Air makes A/C units which can be fitted to such cars. Wish I would have had one of those units back then.

Jim's 1969 Camaro in Stanfield Arizona

—and its motor!

I did get involved in some car "flips" which made me a little money. I would buy cars needing minor repairs, fix them up, and then sell them for a profit. Some of the notable cars I flipped in this manner included a two-door 1966 Buick Special with an aluminum 225 ci V6, a two-door 1968 Impala with a 327 ci V8, and a 1987 Chevy pickup. But the most interesting car was a two-door 1967 Ford Fairlane XL. I bought it for $400, fixed a broken valve spring, and sold it for $1200. I probably should have kept the Fairlane for sure. But I made a good profit on the flip.

I really like GMC trucks. I had a 1988 GMC I drove from 1988-2000, and then another GMC I drove from 2000-2018. Nowadays, I drive a 2018 GMC Canyon with a 2.8 Duramax Turbo. Love it.

Larry's Twin Jet 100 and Suzuki Titan: Jim

When I first met Larry, he was riding a late 60s 100cc Yamaha two-stroke called a Twin Jet. Larry rode his small bike everywhere: to school, to work at Phil's Shoes, down the freeway, and even out in the desert. He crashed the Yamaha all the time on dirt roads and in the desert. It was a street bike with low pipes. He loved that little machine.

A Yamaha Twin Jet 100

Larry and I talked about taking a long motorcycle ride off and on in 1971 and 1972. But his Twin Jet topped out at about 75 mph. It just wouldn't be suitable for very long distances. Although Larry probably would have ridden that Twin Jet anywhere. Anyway, after working part-time for his dad during the summer of 1971 on a gas pipeline project near El Paso, he saved up enough money to buy a Titan 500 right after he got back to Casa Grande.

Larry's folks have the same house in Casa Grande to this day. Back then, Larry stayed in his own room kind of off to the side, sort of part of the carport. I was over there checking out his new 1971 Titan one evening. We went into his room to listen to Pink Floyd or the Beatles or the Hollies when his dad knocked and came in. He had seen the new Suzuki parked on the carport, I guess. He said, "The money must have been burning a hole in your pocket." He was smiling. Larry's dad is a great guy. But anyway, that is the 500 Suzuki Larry would ride to Canada during our 1972 trip. Those things were solid, man.

Early Riding History: Jeff

My folks, sister Julie, and I had lived in Aurora, Nebraska until I was eight years old. Then, in 1962, we moved to the southwest since my dad had an opportunity for a good job in the Phoenix Arizona area. Mom's parents lived in Phoenix, so this helped our transition. I started third grade at Holdeman School in Tempe, Arizona. We lived in Tempe until December of 1965 when we relocated just to the south in Casa Grande. I attended sixth through eleventh grade in Casa Grande, and in many ways, I consider CG to be my hometown. One thing is for sure. Casa Grande is where I learned to ride motorcycles. I also met two of my closest friends, Larry Christopher Jr. and Jim Balding.

Back in 1969 or so, Larry was riding a Yamaha 100 Twin Jet and Jim had an X5 Suzuki 200 motorcycle. I was riding a 1968 Yamaha YR2C 350 Scrambler. (We were certainly two-stroke guys.) Jim and Larry were each slightly older. Jim lived over in Stanfield—his dad was a cotton gin manager. And Larry's dad was a big project pipe liner, an important detail which actually made this trip to Canada story "happen."

Jeff and his Brand-new Yamaha YR2C 350 at the Rancho Del Sol Mobile Home Park, Casa Grande Arizona, March 1, 1970

We had some wonderful short rides back then. Some of the great guys I also rode with included Larry Harwood (Yamaha 305), Dave Logue (Kawasaki Roadrunner 120), and Paco Ollerton (Honda 305 Superhawk, which had a set of lovely chrome megaphone exhausts!). By the way, a few years later, Larry Harwood and Dave Logue were riding Kawasaki Mach IV 750s. The motorcycle culture was "rich" and fun in Casa Grande around 1970. How many times did we blast past Casa Grande Union High School, past the Little Sombrero restaurant, during lunch period?

I screamed down Trekell Road through the cotton fields to and from school. We rode everywhere in the Stanfield, Maricopa, Coolidge, Florence, and Casa Grande area. The back roads and fields were our friends. Once we went to an abandoned Japanese Internment camp just north of Casa Grande. Another time, we travelled down to Picacho Peak and left the pavement for a desert two-track road. I ended up with handfuls of cholla cactus when I spilled my bike in some sand and loose rock. My dad was not happy when I got home, but he did help me straighten out the handlebars. Lesson learned.

Here's another strange thing which happened. In the spring of 1970, I was serving as the student manager for the CGUHS varsity baseball team. One Saturday afternoon, during practice, I parked the Yamaha (appropriately) in the lot adjacent to the ballpark. Some high school girl on a horse came along, did a little spin on the horse, and knocked over my Yamaha. Neither she nor the horse even knew what happened. They trotted off blissfully. Boy, was I mad. Coach Johnson sent me home to cool off. Thankfully, no damage occurred to me or the motorcycle. Or to my brief student managing career.

But things change. In the summer of 1970, I traded in my faithful YR2C for a Kawasaki A7SS Avenger. The rotary valve engine had a little more punch than the Yamaha, and the bright yellow and white gas tank seemed so modern to me. I ripped around Casa Grande on the Avenger the fall of 1970 and spring of 1971. My first "date" was with a pleasant and pretty girl named Elle. I took her to Dell's Pizza and then the Homecoming Dance the fall of 1970 on the Avenger. I don't know if she was impressed with the two-stroke's power.

**Jeff on his Avenger A7SS in Casa Grande. Notice his dad's red
Kawasaki Mach III!**

In May of 1971, our family moved back to Nebraska. I kept the
yellow 350 until about September, then traded it in for a new 1971 blue
Kawasaki 500 Mach III triple at a small Kawasaki dealer near Columbus
Nebraska. The Blue Streak was an absolute jet, but I stayed safe on that
jet except for the time I was rear-ended near York High School by Leroy,
one of my fellow students. After having the rear wheel replaced and re-
spoked by Jerry Hurlbut of iconic Hurlbut Cycle Shop (just north of York
on Highway 81), the Mach III was good to go. And it went nearly 4000
miles in the company of two Suzuki Titans the following summer.

First Section of 1972 Trip from Casa Grande to Nebraska: Jim

A year after Jeff moved to Nebraska, Larry and I decided we'd
take a long motorcycle ride. Larry's dad, Larry Christopher Sr., was
working for Great Plains Construction in Grafton, North Dakota. They
were putting in a big pipeline. We proposed to go up through Nebraska

and pick up Jeff, so to speak, and head north. After seeing Larry's dad for a day or two, the plan was to head on up into Canada, head west a distance, then go down through Montana to Yellowstone. We'd eventually get down to Utah and then back to Arizona. And yes, we made the entire trip without too much trouble. At least Larry and I did. We slept outside most of the time, and we rode through a lot of rain and cold air. But it was fun. I was kind of surprised Jeff's parents let him go all that way, since he just finished high school, but he was eighteen.

Larry and I left Casa Grande on a warm June morning. Our preparations were pretty simple. We tightened our chains, sprayed them with oil, checked air pressure, and filled the oil injection tanks. Each of our bikes had a shoulder-high sissy bar, sort of the fashion back then, and matching square containers for hauling our gear. I had fabricated, for each of us, a heavy-duty cardboard box lined with Masonite and then stuffed the box inside a canvas bag. The box was bolted to the sissy bar. We hauled all our clothes and gear inside those solid waterproof containers. We didn't lose anything, either. Unlike Jeff. More on his issues later.

We just carried sleeping bags and clothes, pretty much, and chain oil and a few tools. I had an industrial strength Diamond Chain, still new in the box, and a chain breaker, but we never needed it. We didn't carry any tents, but I had a big tarp stuffed in there. We only stayed in a motel two nights—once in Watertown, South Dakota and the other time in Provo, Utah.

Our first big destination, a couple of days out, would be Jeff's house in York, Nebraska, on Highway 81. We headed up I-10 (a fairly new stretch of freeway at the time) to Phoenix and then picked up I-17 to Flagstaff. Those two 500s really moaned going up the long hills into Flag. They were happy to get out of the heat! And that quick change in scenery as you get higher, from desert to forest, is just magnificent. After some lunch, we transitioned on to Highway 89 and into the Four Corners area toward Tuba City. We eventually got onto Highway 160. Somehow, we ended up just east of Durango, Colorado. We rolled out our mats and sleeping bags and slept in a nice, lush green field. The night was chilly but bearable. Durango is at about 6500 feet elevation, and this was still June. Come to think of it, we spent quite a few nights in sleeping bags at high elevation (or in the rain) on this trip. When we woke up, we were surrounded by sheep. I never saw any of them the previous evening when we were unloading our gear, but they were everywhere at daybreak.

One of my memories is how cold it was when we made it through Wolf Creek Pass on Highway 160 after leaving Durango early in the morning. Seems like the air was cold half the trip until we returned to Arizona.

We meandered around, got to Walsenburg, then headed up to Denver eventually on I-25, and picked up old Highway 6 eastbound. Larry and I slept on some picnic tables near Stirling, Colorado our second night out. No rain and not as chilly. The next day we rolled peacefully into Nebraska. Larry and I noticed western Nebraska looked a lot like eastern Colorado: rolling hills, bluffs, cattle, and kind of scattered agriculture. But central Nebraska is flat, very green in the summer, and heavily cultivated.

We wanted to stay off the freeways as much as we could, so we avoided I-80. Eventually, we came to the Highway 6/81 junction and headed north to Jeff's house in York, Nebraska. We spent a couple of days doing some maintenance work on the Suzukis, eating his mom's good cooking, and more or less hanging out. I remember Jeff's dad was starting work an aircraft down in the basement, a homebuilt plane called a Bowers Fly Baby. We slept down in that basement and had quick access to a good hot shower. Just before we left for North Dakota, I remember Jeff's mom telling me how neat the "packaged" loads on our motorcycles looked, and how Jeff's was haphazardly strapped together.

After Leaving York, Nebraska: Jeff

Our plan for the first leg of our trip was to ride from York, Nebraska up Highway 81 to Grafton, North Dakota, where Larry's dad was helping install 142 miles of new gas pipeline in the Jamison-Grafton area. Highway 81 is and was a major thoroughfare across the central United States. We took it (mostly) all the way north to Pembina, North Dakota, and then crossed into Canada. As we moved north out of York, space opened some and the sky got bigger, but the scenery in Nebraska, South Dakota, and southern North Dakota was very similar: small farms and green fields.

When we left York on a humid June 10th morning, we had no idea what was ahead of us in terms of weather.

I had made several trips to Columbus and Norfolk, Nebraska during the past year. Those cities were in my "neighborhood." For me, I would say, the trip really began when we eased out of Norfolk (which is, by the way, comedian Johnny Carson's hometown). Most of the passage through Nebraska during the morning was calm and pleasant. Those two-stokes were howling beautifully. We hustled up the concrete slab through Columbus and Norfolk. Later, we took a little jog on Highway 121 over to Gavin's Point Dam, on the Missouri River bordering South Dakota. Water was splashing and dancing through the spillways—a very beautiful sight but portentous. The dam, built in 1957, is an earth and chalk-filled structure which backs up Lewis and Clark Lake. We saw some people fishing for catfish just below the dam.

As mentioned earlier, the morning was very hot and humid. (A very big rain was moving in from the north and west of us.) Jim and Larry decide to go for a swim in the Big Mo river. They complained about smelling like two-stoke-smoke from my Mach III. I think they just wanted to be able to say they went swimming in the Missouri River. They changed clothes behind some trees and put some shorts on and then splashed around in the muddy water for a few minutes. Larry took a bar of soap in the river with him. I sort of kept an eye on things while they were swimming and goofing around. After a while, they got out and dried off and put their riding clothes back on so we could head out. We learned the road over the dam was closed all day for some maintenance, so we returned to Highway 81 on the 121 and crossed the river into Yankton, South Dakota via the Meridian Bridge.

Spillway at Gavin's Point Dam
(Photo courtesy South Dakota Tourism)

That bridge is actually rather famous. Built in 1919, it is a double decker, and was originally designed for both autos and trains. Jim and I both mentioned later how spooky it was crossing the Missouri River on a bridge with a "cheese grater" roadway. Our bikes wobbled along on the uneven metal surfaces, and we could see the Missouri River churning away below us.

Meridian Bridge
(Photo courtesy National Park Service)

Rain became a big issue very soon after we entered South Dakota. This was the grim year of the 1972 Rapid City Floods. According to the National Weather Service (NWS), "On the evening of June 9, 1972, heavy thunderstorms caused devastating flash flooding throughout Rapid City and the eastern foothills of the Black Hills—destroying homes, vehicles, businesses, and bridges, and claiming 238 lives." While we were far east of Rapid City, wide and deep and dark rain bands caught us and really slowed us down that afternoon. I remember seeing outhouses, or porta-potties, banging up against the bridge when we crossed the swollen Big Sioux River in Watertown, South Dakota. (Talk about pollution. Hah!) I guess that did it. We were tired of being wet, hydroplaning, and the fierce storms. Soaked from the heavy rain, we found a warm and dry motel room... the last motel room we would see for several days. Sometimes a hot shower really is priceless!

The next morning was clear and cool as we headed toward Grafton, North Dakota, but the rain wasn't finished with us yet. That rainstorm cycle would "haunt us" the next couple of days. More on the precipitation later.

The prairie states are similar but different. As we moved further north, we noticed the sky getting bigger and the gradual "stretch" of landscapes. Because it was June, the crop growth in South Dakota and North Dakota wasn't as far along as in a "southern" place like Nebraska. The plants were much shorter, or the fields were still bare in the Dakotas. And the morning temps were cool and very damp after the recent rains.

Grafton, North Dakota: Jeff

We spent the better part of two days in Grafton. Highlights of the stay included visiting the pipeline construction site where Larry's dad was working, sleeping overnight out in the fenced-in area where the construction company kept their equipment, and almost being tossed out of a bar and grill when the bartender, a fellow who looked like Archie Bunker except with a full head of hair, wouldn't give me a beer. Larry's dad had ordered up a round for all of us. "How old are you, son?" the barkeep asked me with forcefulness, noting my peach fuzz complexion. "Eighteen," I bleated in a confused manner. "Thought so. I can't serve

20

you, and you can't stay at this bar."

Not too embarrassed, we migrated to a table and had steaks. I managed to get an iced tea. Happily. Larry's dad was very generous, and we had a great time. Installing a gas pipeline is a major construction project, and the machinery, scope of the endeavor, and professionalism of the workers were all very impressive. Fortunately, no rain. One rather odd thing happened. Somewhere around Grafton, we crossed some railroad tracks. Not long after, Larry pulled over on his Titan with a flat tire. Crazy, but there was a big splinter, or piece of wood, from a railroad tie which had punctured the tire. A problem fairly easily fixed but....

After the second night sleeping in the construction yard, and waking up damp from a heavy dew, we tightened and oiled our chains, and set out the forty or fifty miles to the Canadian border just north of Pembina.

At the Canadian Border and Winnipeg: Jim

Of course, we weren't hippies or outlaw bikers or anything, but those Royal Mounted Police or border guards weren't very friendly. The welcoming Canadians didn't treat me very well. They saw I had a bottle of allergy medicine, so they tore into all my stuff and made a big mess. Of course, they didn't find anything illegal, but they killed a lot of time. A lot. And they didn't repack my gear. There was a big mess of tarps and socks and tools all over the table. What's more, after they unpacked all my belongings, they didn't even look at the other guys' stuff. Hour detained! !@#$!

When we left, I was so mad I wound up my Titan's engine (wah wah wah wah) and left a black streak on the pavement. I was probably lucky not to get arrested. I also came to realize gas cost more up there (Imperial Gallons). And we got turned away from a hamburger joint when we tried to spend American money. Hungry still, and increasingly grumpy, we had to go to a bank and exchange some of our US dollars for Canadian money. Jeff told me he still has a Canadian dollar or two from our trip.

Later, a twelve-year-old red-headed kid rode up on a minibike while we were eating at an A&W drive-in somewhere in Winnipeg. He looked at the license plate on my bike and asked, "You rode them sons-a-bitches all the way from Arizona?" Some cute girls were eyeballing us from a convertible, but nothing happened. Welcome to Canada.

West on Highway Manitoba 2: Jeff

Winnipeg kind of reminded me of Sioux Falls, South Dakota or Lincoln, Nebraska. It was a big city, but not too big, with commercial connections to energy, industry, and agriculture. We didn't have much trouble getting around. After lunch at the A & W, Larry pointed us westward down Highway Manitoba 2. Our goal was to head to Weyburn, Saskatchewan, about 400-500 miles away, spend the night in a motel, and gradually veer back into the US and find Plentywood, Montana. The day was sunny and pleasant when we left Winnipeg early in the afternoon, but the good weather vibes sure didn't last for very long.

The Manitoba 2 was a narrow paved two-lane road back in those days, and we were travelling across prairie and farming country. Heavy rain started, and visibility was an issue. We could barely see anything off to the side of the road in the cloudburst. A couple of hours passed, and conditions became really bad. An oncoming Greyhound Bus, or its Canadian equivalent, created a wall of water as we met it blasting towards us. I should have had a surfboard. Seriously, we were nearly splashed off the road.

Somewhere out there a couple hundred miles or so west of Winnipeg, we knew we had to seek shelter. The sky was dark, we were soaked, and our machines were sputtering. Suddenly, we came upon a group of big fifty-foot-high cylindrical galvanized steel grain bins, pulled over, and tried to open the door at the base of one of them just to get inside. Crazy idea. The bin was full of corn, which started spilling out on the ground as we slowly raised the door just a few inches. We quickly forced the door shut. The pounding rain kept falling. So did our spirits.

We returned to the highway and, fortunately, just a few miles further, spotted an abandoned farmhouse on the north side of Manitoba 2. Boards and shingles, nails, and pieces of junk were scattered everywhere in the rutted gravel and mud driveway. (Thinking back, we were lucky nobody discovered a flat tire when we went out to reload the next morning.) We easily found the crooked, unlocked front door, grabbed our dripping baggage, and found our way inside the spooky old house. I was so glad to get in out of the rain. The poor bikes had to stay outside, though. I had nightmares all night about a crushing wall of water and a rusting chain.

I did have the good sense earlier to wrap my sleeping gear in a plastic trash bag, so it was still dry. We sort of made our beds wherever we could. I put my sleeping bag on an old door resting on the floor, which was kind of a hard surface, but the arrangement worked out ok. The inside of the house was in disarray: dry wall, lumber, cabinets, dishes, old broken toys, and debris lay scattered everywhere. But the roof didn't seem to leak, and we stayed dry all night.

The kitchen had one of those old four-burner cast iron stoves with lion paw feet. Always resourceful Larry built a fire for heat and for cooking a can or two of soup. Plenty of wood was scattered around, for sure. We didn't burn the place down, but the chimney pipe smoked a little. And some crusty pigeon manure which was stuck to the top of the old stove started smoking and really stunk up the place. We were quite cozy, although our new quarters were smelly for quite a while.

I slept very well, even though a rat or mouse ran over my face a time or two, and probably a spider or roach. We could hear disenfranchised rodents scurrying and scratching everywhere. Perhaps they were glad to have the warmth of the stove.

Next morning, the sun shone brightly. The new day was clear, cool, and damp once again. We oiled our chains (thickly) and packed gear and rambled to Weyburn for breakfast. Larry was adamant he needed a plate of eggs. We found an interesting place right along the road and had a good meal. Not long after, though, as we were leaving town, Larry turned a little too sharply at an intersection and dumped his motorcycle. No damage. Must have been the eggs.

About this time, also, I noticed a worrisome, peculiar metallic zing-zing sound emanating from the engine's clutch housing on my Mach III. The weird sound was most pronounced at idle, but I could hear it, or so I thought, at all speeds. Not good. Jim and Larry listened to the emanation and made some remark like, "You should have bought a Suzuki!"

**An old water tower in Weyburn
(Image courtesy *Wikipedia* Commons)**

Montana: Jeff.

We were careful to pick an "unguarded/no checkpoint" when crossing/reentering the US. We didn't want another interrogation. That part of Canada and Montana look very similar. We just rolled across a line of latitude on a two-lane paved road and were back in the USA. Ahh!

Somewhere between Plentywood, Montana and the I-94 Junction to the south, around June 15, we were rolling through a series of hills and low mountains on a very rough highway. The day was warm and dry for a change. Our motorcycles were howling on the open road, and we were making time. At some point, I happened to notice in my mirror that one of my strapped-on backpacks was missing. I saw a gap in my luggage pile. Ahrr!

Great. I motioned to Jim and Larry to pull over. After explaining the situation to them, we formulated a plan of action. I would back track about five miles to the very rough and bouncy section of road we just came through and hopefully find the backpack. They would wait for me. I took a quick look for oncoming traffic, made a U-turn, and rolled up to about 120 mph on the 500cc Kawasaki, heading back to the northeast and a ridge of hills.

About three minutes later, I noticed flashing lights in my mirror. A Montana Highway Patrol cruiser had caught up to me. Great again. The day was getting worse. I pulled over, frightened and nervous. Wearing sunglasses and very muscular, the patrolman walked up to me after I parked on the shoulder, with his hand on his gun holster, and asked me why I made that U-turn when I saw him coming and took off. I told him my story. Not quite satisfied, he told me to wait there while he went back to call in my license and registration info. I felt like a suspect on the old *Adam 12* TV show! (But this couldn't be a 211 or a 459!) I heard him talking into the radio while he stood outside his car and kept an eye on me. He was repeating my license plate numbers. Well, I soon learned nothing "bad" came back from headquarters. Did I get a speeding ticket? No. Why not? Well, no speed limit was posted in such places throughout Montana at the time. I guess 118 mph (at which he said he clocked me) was acceptable. The proper phrase was "reasonable and prudent."

The officer actually helped me look around for the lost pack for a while, and then we parted ways amicably. He was a very nice man. I never did find my khaki-colored Boy Scout pack. After riding up and down about five miles of highway a few times, I gave up and returned to the other lads who were waiting for me. Larry had made a cup of coffee and looked reflective. Jim was anxious to get going. The really bad news? I lost my camera (and the first third of the trip's pictures) along with socks, t-shirts, chain oil, and cans of soup, chili, and beans. Jim was kind enough to loan me the money to buy a replacement camera, a Kodak Instamatic, in Billings the next day.

A Kodak Instamatic from the era. It used a cube for a flash.

I felt bad about the whole deal. I still do forty-nine years later. At least I wasn't arrested. Jim later said some "old bum" or hitchhiker more and likely felt rich when he found my backpack. Great. Certainly, there was a delicious meal in canned chili or soup in there, besides the camera. Larry had warned me back in York that I needed a better system to strap and pack my bags onto my motorcycle. They had those wonderful industrial grade boxes to hold their stuff. I had a bunch of bags, packs, and bungie cords all hanging together. He was right. I should have packed better. My mom tried to tell me the same thing!

Later, we zoomed down I-94 toward Billings. After eating at a Miles City, Montana drive-in about dusk, we found our way out to a clean, shaded rest area a little bit south and west of town, just off the freeway, and decided to spend the night on, or under, some picnic tables. The sunset was pleasant, and we were happy to finish the day's long ride. We were quite pleased to be back in the states, to tell you the truth.

Two things memorable happened that night: One, a big thunderstorm came up which about washed us away (that's how we ended up under the tables). Sure was a good thing Jim brought along some tarps. Two, Jim discovered black widow spiders like the underside of picnic tables in Montana. The storm cleared out sometime after midnight, and we were able to get a mostly restful sleep. No police officer or deputy came by to see what we were up to. Do you think such naïve, freedom-loving camping practices would be tolerated in the 21st century?

By the time we arrived at Billings, Montana the next day, I was feeling worn out and dispirited. We stopped for an early lunch and visited a Kawasaki shop to get an assessment of the zing-zing noise emanating from the three-cylinder engine. The friendly service manager was good enough to listen to my idling machine. He was unsure of the problem. "Might be a clutch issue," he said matter-of-factly. "Doesn't sound like a crank or con rod problem. We'd have to tear it down to find out. Might be the release bearing running off-center, an out-of-whack shaft, or a bad pilot bearing. How far do you have to go?" Reflecting, and calculating rapidly, I replied, "About 2500 miles." "Oh," he said. You'll probably make it okay. We couldn't get to it for a few days anyway. Your shifting might get iffy. Take 'er easy the rest of the trip." Comforting. Do you think I listened to the motor constantly after that?

But you know what? He was right. I did make it back… zing-zing noise and all.

Billings Montana: Jim

I remember getting kind of aggravated in the beautiful city of Billings. We arrived in town about 10:30 am and stopped at a Kawasaki dealer. Jeff told the story about his bike. We did pick up some chain oil at the dealership because the constant rain had caused us to use up most of our initial supply. I think we bought a few bottles of two-stroke oil, also. Then, later, we kept riding around Billings looking for a place to get a camera. See above. Hah. After an hour or two, we found an Instamatic at a mall. The Kodak wasn't exactly like the one Jeff lost, but it was pretty close. Seems like the buttons or case were a different color. Also, Larry stopped to buy a loaf of bread somewhere. I remember the loaf got kind of smashed up when he crammed into his pack.

I'm not sure why he wanted that bread. Hmm. Every morning,

before sunrise, whether we were camping or in a motel, Larry would crash around and get out his little two-cup coffee pot and some coffee and a Sterno fuel heater. He had to have his coffee way early. No matter what he was doing, or where he was located, Larry loved a before-sunrise cup of coffee. Maybe the loaf of bread was for toast.

Billings to Yellowstone: Jim

Larry was the chief navigator for our trip. He had a notebook and all kinds of maps stuffed into the canvas box on his bike. Larry was really good with road atlases and directions. Maybe this was because his family moved all over the country working on pipelines when he was growing up. Jeff and I just kind of followed along. The two of us were very comfortable with Larry's trip leadership. Larry knew where we were going, knew the best route, and we trusted him completely. (If you wish, you can check out Appendix A below, at the end of this Canada trip story, which describes the highways we took and the places we stayed during our trip.)

After we left Billings that afternoon, with a brand-new camera, chain oil, and a fresh loaf of bread, we headed down the Beartooth Highway, or Highway 212, toward Red Lodge on the northeast corner of Yellowstone. The scenery on 212 is magnificent: lots of water, canyons, and trees.

A Highway 212 View!

What I remember best is going through Beartooth Pass at about 11,000 feet elevation. We were travelling in the middle of June by now, but snow was still piled everywhere. And it was cold. Way cold. That highway was like a black ribbon through a snow canyon where plows had cleaned the highway.

Larry having fun in the snow at Beartooth Pass. Notice the snowplow in the background.

29

Jeff (in stylish black 1970s Naugahyde jacket) and Jim at Beartooth Pass. Do they look warm? No, Jeff did not appear in *The Day the Earth Stood Still* movie.

We made it into Yellowstone late in the afternoon, but the days were very long at that time of year and plenty of sunlight remained. I am sure we exceeded the speed limit as we motored through the National Park. We did see Yellowstone Lake and Old Faithful and all kinds of elk and bear and tourists milling around alongside the road. Quickly. We finally stopped to camp near a stream. I guess it might have been the Yellowstone River. We were near a sign that said plainly— *"No Camping Allowed-Bear Danger!"* Not long after we started unloading our gear, Larry pointed down the river about a hundred yards and said, "Look. There's a bear standing in the water. See him?" Jeff squinted in the direction Larry had pointed but didn't say anything. I took a look and gave my assessment. "Looks like an old stump to me, Larry." I sure didn't see any bear. We kept working away at setting up our camp. A minute or two later, Larry turned to me and said, "Hey Jim, your stump just got up and walked away!"

We ate a sack of four-hour-old hamburgers we had picked up somewhere along the road and maybe heated up some soup or chili. But it was really cold that night. We didn't notice anybody or any animals until morning. Fortunately, we didn't see any Forest Rangers. Larry was up early making coffee, and we stoked up the campfire for warmth. I did observe a bear or two ambling around in the distance while we were packing up our blankets and sleeping bags.

As soon as it was warm enough, we hauled out of there in a cloud of blue smoke and headed down Highway 191 toward the Grand Tetons. Soon, the Tetons stood, a giant sawtooth mountain wall, off to the west. This was another really picturesque area which we pretty much zoomed though, stopping only a couple of times to take pictures or get gas.

The Grand Tetons in 1972

Around Jackson, Wyoming, we picked up Highway 89 and headed toward Montpelier, Idaho and Bear Lake. The scenery was simply magnificent. We took a little jog around the Lake on Highway 30 to Route 16 down to Evanston, and we moved on to I-80 and backtracked a little into Provo, Utah.

Bear Lake Idaho/Utah Border (courtesy Visit Idaho.org)
Provo, Utah: Jim

The three of us arrived in Provo late that afternoon after trekking through Evanston on Utah 16 and avoiding the Ogden and Salt Lake City rush hour traffic. Somewhere, as we were coming into Provo, Jeff got into a lane that was closed by orange highway cones. Larry and I noticed he was sort of in a jam and boxed in, so we stopped and waited for him to maneuver out of there. Nothing happened, but he should have been paying more attention.

When we were gassing up for the next day's ride, I noticed I had just about completely worn out the rear tire on my Titan. The thing was shot, cracked up, just about worn clear through. We went to some motorcycle shop and found a replacement. It fit but was not what I wanted. I got a Goodyear Super Eagle, the kind of tire which is sort of flat on the bottom and has square sides. (Similar to the one I put on that Hummer many years before!) There isn't much of a curve to the tread wall or anything. You see such tires on choppers and bobbers sometimes. Well, I couldn't corner worth a d*** but it was a decent tire. I installed it in the alley behind the motel where we decided to stay. Or allowed us to stay. The first place we visited had a message on the sign out front: No Motorcycles Allowed.

I remember thinking, while installing my new tire, that I probably wasted about 2000 miles of tire tread back at the North Dakota/Canadian border crossing. The angry but cathartic burn-out most certainly caused the premature demise of my tire and plenty of extra work.

By the way, that new Super Eagle tire lasted a long time. I just couldn't corner very well.

Provo to Page: Jeff

We travelled south from Provo, Utah to Page, Arizona down Highway 89, a trip of about 350 miles. The southern Utah drive is very scenic as the highway is situated between the Manti-La Sal National Forest and the Fishlake National Forest. Utah, as mentioned earlier, is a very beautiful state. But our tendency was to roll along at 70-75 mph and stop periodically only for gas and food. We were riders rather than tourists, and the tone of the trip changed once we were south of Moab. Larry and Jim wanted to get back home. I wanted to get off that Mach III for a couple of days before my last leg of the trip back to Nebraska. Even so, we pulled off the road occasionally at a scenic overlook to take in the view.

I had a rather personal mystical moment when we were still a few miles north of Kanab, Utah. We stopped by a pond, which was nestled against a rock formation, sort of a cliff, to stretch and rest a few minutes. The water surface reached back into a shallow cave. Nice shade trees surrounded the pond, and the water was very clear. I noticed some large golden carp swimming in the shallow water, and suddenly remembered I had been at this same wonderful place many years ago, back in 1965, when my parents and sister and I stopped here on a family vacation. Back then, we fed the fish, and we also "visited" with a beautiful horse who was behind the fence framing the property. We were on our way northward to see our relations, Jerolyn and Rich Oswald, in Bountiful, Utah. The four of us were riding in the same 1962 Rambler Classic (three-on-the-tree, straight six, overdrive, no A/C) that had brought us to Arizona from Nebraska three years earlier.

I doubt if the same fish were swimming around in 1972 when Jim, Larry, and I stopped by, but it was the same pond. For sure. Also, I didn't see the horse. Wish he'd been there....

Nose of the Rambler *Classic* at the lovely Utah pond site in 1965

Glen Canyon Dam and Page Arizona: Jeff

We arrived in Page, Arizona, still on Highway 89, about midafternoon. There wasn't enough time left in the day to make it to Phoenix or Casa Grande, so we decided to tour the new Glen Canyon Dam and then camp south of town a bit. Page was more or less built, or developed, because of the dam's construction during the 1960s. The three of us took a nice tour of the dam, a dam tour much like the one described in the Chevy Chase movie *Vegas Vacation*. We didn't get into any Clark Griswold trouble. We enjoyed riding the elevator, seeing the power plant turbines, and learning about the dam's construction in Glen Canyon. Larry and Jim had Arizona fishing licenses but no fishing gear along, so they weren't able to fish.

Larry and Jim on Dam Tour

I also remember quite a bit of construction activity was going on out in the desert near Page. The Navajo Generating Plant was being built at that time. (The coal fired plant, unable to meet emissions standards, was decommissioned recently, in November 2019). The dam is still holding back the Colorado River.

After eating at a fast-food place in Page (such establishments were a common source of nourishment, good or bad, for us on this trip), we set up camp just off Highway 89 under some menacing transmission lines. I am sure the tower-supported lines came from the dam's power station. Well, all night long, those lines hummed and sparked and snapped. Jim to this day believes the electrical waves may have altered our brains permanently.

**Notice transmission lines overhead in this early morning photo of
our Page campsite.**

Camping South of Page: Jim

Who knows why we picked that particular spot to camp? We must
have arrived there after dark. Why else would we sleep under snapping-
crackling electrical powerlines all night? I remember the sand was really
soft, and we had to find a rock or two to put the side stands on so our bikes
wouldn't tip over. We slept up on a dune. You can tell the picture above
was taken from a slightly higher elevation. I'm surprised nobody got
stung by a scorpion out there. Jeff saw several of them by the light of our
campfire. Also, notice, in the picture above, the coffee pot is already
packed onto Larry's bike. He was ready to go! You can see some two-
stroke smoke being emitted from the middle motorcycle in the photo. Off
in the distance, you can detect some more smoke or dust. Maybe that was
the Navajo Generating Plant under construction.

Page to Flagstaff Arizona: Jeff

We continued down Highway 89, passing just to the east of the Grand Canyon, on our 130 mile or so jaunt to Flagstaff. We jetted through the communities of Cameron and Gray Mountain, pausing only for gas, before picking up I-40 briefly a few miles outside of Flagstaff. Funny, I had no idea as we stopped in Flag to get a bite to eat that I would spend most of the summers in the 1980s there as a grad student at Northern Arizona University. But we weren't interested in academics at that moment. Not a bit. Larry was ready to roll! Jim and I were simply beat.

Phoenix: Jeff

Larry was in a huge hurry to get home to Casa Grande and see his girlfriend. Jim and I occasionally lost sight of him after we left Flagstaff, the three of us screaming southward on I-17. We'd catch up to him, then he'd pull away. I think we finally gave up and settled on 70 mph. Larry was really rolling down the freeway.

After Jim and I arrived in Phoenix, on a very warm late June day, we turned off the freeway and headed over to my maternal grandparents' house. They lived near 44th and Indian School. Larry surely had arrived in Casa Grande, forty or so miles to the southeast, by then. Jim spent an hour or two cooling off in the A/C and then left for Stanfield. That was the last I saw of Jim and Larry on that trip. I was pretty tired, I guess, and did not ride down to Casa Grande to see them or any of my old friends. In hindsight, that was an error in judgement.

But I had only been away from Casa Grande for a year. Also, the Mach III was still making those funny zing-zing engine noises, and I didn't want to stress the machine in the heat.

Home: Jim

It didn't take us long to get from Flagstaff to Phoenix down I-17.

Larry was in a super hurry to see his girlfriend (soon-to-be-wife) Dolores. He flattened on that Titan and was going 90 miles an hour down the freeway most of the time. We kept up with him for a while. And it was getting hotter and hotter as we dropped down into the desert. Flagstaff, at over 7000 ft elevation, has pine trees and cool temps most of the year. Phoenix is a furnace in the summer. Always.

Here's an interesting fact I should have mentioned earlier. We didn't carry any water with us on the entire trip. Or at least very little. Larry must have had some available for making coffee. We drank sodas and water at all the places we stopped to eat, and sometimes coffee with Larry in the morning. I guess it was so cold and wet most of the time we didn't miss it. Except for that last 150 miles or so from Flagstaff to Phoenix.

Well, when I got back to Stanfield, I just went into the cotton gin manager's house where I was living (by myself at the time) and cranked down that A/C. I probably set the thermostat at 60 degrees. After being cold most of the last ten days, that heat was just about unbearable. I took a long, long nap in the cold air. But I was pretty young and bounced back quickly. Later in the evening, I headed over to Casa Grande to fool around.

Riding Solo from Tempe Arizona to Vaughn, New Mexico: Jeff

I was ready to head home. The big ride, I thought, was over. I had been to Canada and Yellowstone and taken a dam tour. I don't know if I was fearful of going those last 1200 miles by myself or not. But I called home on the phone, while in Phoenix, and asked my dad to ride down to the Guymon, Oklahoma area to meet me so we could ride the last 400 miles or back to York together. He was happy to make the trip, but we scheduled the event on a Friday/Saturday so he wouldn't miss too much work. He had a really nice green CB 450 Honda at the time.

Anyway, while in the Phoenix area, I spent a day and night with my grandparents, Dr. Ray and Virginia Reynolds, mostly lounging, swimming in their pool, eating home-cooked food, and enjoying the air conditioning. My Grandma Reynolds made great fried chicken. After goodbyes, I headed over to Tempe to see my aunt and uncle, Deanna and Steve Cooley. I did a little maintenance work on the Kawasaki: tire pressure, chain oil, oil injection fill. I enjoyed a good Mexican dinner cooked by Steve, caught up on family news, spent the night, and started the grinding 1200-mile trip back to Nebraska the following day.

In general, I rode solo on Highway US 60 from Tempe to Vaughn, New Mexico (500 miles); Highway US 54 through Dalhart, Texas (where I met up with my dad… story follows) and Liberal, Kansas (325 miles); then, a few miles past Kingman, Kansas, we headed north on Highway 14 into Nebraska (200 miles). We paused for a time in Aurora, Nebraska, to visit with my grandparents, then "sleepwalked" east down Highway US 34 (the last 20 miles) to York and home.

I left my aunt and uncle's in Tempe, Arizona about 6 am on a warm, overcast, humid late June morning. Typically, the rainy monsoon season starts around July 4th in southern Arizona. That particular morning had a pretentious, heavy weather feeling. June is usually bright and sunny. That day was gray.

I rolled down Highway 60, the Apache Trail in the East Valley, and headed past the iconic Grand Hotel in Apache Junction. I cruised up through the 2000 ft. elevation Gonzales Pass and gassed up in Globe about 30 miles further down the road. My trip took me through the wonderful hairpin curves of the Salt River Canyon before climbing into the forests of the Mogollon Rim.

I remember thinking it was a little strange to be riding alone. Did I see apparitions or wishful images of my smiling companions in my mirrors? Did I miss Larry's coffee or Jim's Super Eagle tire? No, but I certainly thought about them and missed the comradery. And I envied them because they were home and stationary. I was howling down a two-lane road through Cibecue to Show Low and beyond under threatening skies. Also, I kept thinking about that zing-zing sound which seemed more evident, but that might have been in my head.

Hungry and energized, I stopped in Show Low, Arizona for more gas and had breakfast at a café. (That café is still open in 2021. We now call the place affectionately the "Low Eave" café because the edge of the roof near the front door is only about 5 feet off the ground. I walked into the eave once back on a later motorcycle ride in 2011. Ouch.)

Shortly thereafter, during the forty miles or so between Show Low and Springville, Arizona, I was caught in a brutal downpour and hailstorm. The weather really set it. I was soaked immediately. Were these angry and freezing rainstorms following me all over North America?

Cold and wet once again, I stopped in Springerville for coffee and dried off a little. When the sun came out, two hours later, I oiled my chain and hit the road and soon entered western New Mexico. But the delay kept me from my goal of reaching Tucumcari, New Mexico later that day. Oh well.

I had a good tail wind as the skies cleared and the road moved in a gentle easterly direction. Highway 60 winds through some very beautiful country and passes through the interesting communities of Pie Town, Quemado, and Magdalena. Near Socorro, I turned up I-25 and rode north for a few miles before exiting and getting back on Highway 60. My day's ride was about done because of the earlier rain delay. I passed through Mountainair (many years later, on a different ride with my dad, I was able to find a drive chain for my RD 400 in Mountainair—a trip saving find, I might add!) and arrived in Vaughn, New Mexico (where I would junction to Highway 54 the next day).

I decided to get a motel in Vaughn—found a nice place with an adjoining café. Beat but prudent, I tightened the Mach III's chain, oiled it up, filled the oil injection tank, took a shower, had a great hamburger at the café, and called my dad. We cooked up the following scheme:

1. He would ride his CB 450 down to Guymon, Oklahoma the next day and spend the night at a motel on the west side of town.
2. I would go to Dalhart, Texas and get a motel.
3. We would each have separate leisurely breakfasts and leave our "spots" at 7 am local time. Our motel rooms would only be about seventy-five

miles apart. But we were concerned about predicted late afternoon tornados, hail, and all that.

We would look for each other on Highway 54 the next morning... somewhere around the Texas/Oklahoma border.

Then, after a successful rendezvous, we would return to Nebraska and be home by dusk.

The plan basically worked. You must remember, there were no cell phones in those days. We simply set up a schedule over a sketchy landline and then just acted with a simple faith that things would come together.

Vaughn, New Mexico to Aurora, Nebraska: Jeff.

The following day, I pulled into Dalhart, Texas shortly past noon, after being rained on again near Tucumcari, New Mexico. That part of Texas has two dominant features: the sprawling XIT Ranch and bent trees everywhere. The trees have a permanent bend, it seems, from the west wind which is always blowing.

Not long after acquiring a motel room (no I didn't have reservations for this or any motel on the trip), I pushed my grimy 500 over to a nearby carwash (so as not to heat up the engine) and gave the machine a good cleaning. I was beat. I remember having a bowl of chili from the nearby café and watching rabbit ear antennae TV in my motel room. That night, another big thunderstorm, as expected, rolled through, but I was safe under the covers. I was quite happy not to be under a picnic table or in an abandoned house. Plus, the motel was also rodent and pigeon free.

After a pleasant night's sleep, I had a nice, unrushed breakfast of hash browns, bacon, and scrambled eggs (surely, I thought of Larry Christopher at that moment) about 6 am at the cafe and then walked back and loaded up my machine for the last haul. After performing the usual pre-ride chores, I let the bike warm up and rode over to a Conoco station for gas. The analog gas pump clattered and rattled as I put in two gallons of fuel. At 7:05, I was on the road and the sky was sunny.

The Mach III's engine was still making weird sounds, but my

confidence was building. I felt like I was almost home! Miles slipped by. The Texas air was fresh and damp. I had to dodge a few puddles. Man, I was focused. I kept my eyes peeled on the highway and the shoulder, looking at every turnout, every intersection for my dad. I kept heading down the road. I looked behind every tree, every grain elevator, at every gas station parking lot—everywhere—for him and his green and gold 1971 CB 450. Then, somewhere between Stratford, Texas and Texhoma on the Oklahoma border, we met each other on the road. Sort of. I was behind a big rig truck, and he was behind a big rig truck, and we just managed to spot each other as we howled around a sweeping curve. I remember seeing his brake light go in my mirror as he pulled over, and I also came to a quick stop. After all our planning, we had almost missed each other. Hah. That would have been funny. We laughed back then and still laugh now. Fortunes of the road, I guess.

But our plan worked. We spent a few minutes comparing notes and then headed to Texhoma and Liberal, finally finding our way north, later in the afternoon, on Highway 14. The return trip was quite uneventful... just a dad on his Honda and his son on a Kawasaki putting closure to the lad's 4000-mile ride. The warm, fragrant, humid Midwest air seemed wonderful to me—very refreshing and familiar. I was paying less and less attention to the zing-zing noise.

Jeff and his dad, Doyle Ross, meet on the Windy Plains of the Texas Panhandle.
Notice Jeff's snazzy Kawasaki Green Racing outfit.

I do remember feeling quite triumphant as we crossed into Nebraska and rode the last forty or fifty miles up Highway 14 past familiar farms, fields, and ponds. The small communities of Superior, Nelson, and Clay Center, Nebraska seemed welcoming, almost glad to see me. My dad and I stopped in Aurora at my grandparents' home (SE and Blanche Ross) for an hour or so to get refreshed and to let the family see we had survived the trip. We wanted to get back to York, our home twenty miles or so to the east, before dark.

Jeff at his grandparent's house in Aurora, Nebraska near the end of the trip.

From Aurora, we took Highway 34 and passed through the communities of Hampton and Bradshaw. I remember the "final ride" seemed like a long, long twenty miles. I had gone approximately 4000 miles the last two weeks. Finally, we got back on Highway 81 for a few minutes, headed south into York, and then we were suddenly at our house on Edison Avenue.

I had turned eighteen the previous February, and now, in June, I had just completed quite a trip. Cool. Great ride.

Postscript-The Zing-Zing Noise and the new R5C Yamaha: Jeff

I spent a day or two cleaning my bike and putting stuff away and probably taking a nap or two. Then I rode out to Hurlbut Cycle Shop, a Triumph and Yamaha dealer just a few miles north of York on Highway 81. The Hurlbuts were (and are to this day) great friends. I thought I would have Jerry Hurlbut, an expert two-stroke mechanic, take a look at the Mach III and see if he could fix the bothersome, noisy non- issue with the clutch or whatever it was.

Then, great change. While he took my Kawasaki for a ride, I noticed a new black and orange 1972 Yamaha 350 R5C in the showroom.

Jerry, upon returning, asked me a few questions, and quietly told me he thought he noticed an issue with a bushing or bearing needle or release assembly or something. Long story short—he said it was easily fixable. But I was taken with that black and orange R5. Perhaps unbelievably, I committed to trading it my Mach III 500cc for the R5 350cc soon after. The deal was consummated in early July. I had loved the fierce Mach III, but there was just something about that Yamaha.

The next summer in 1973 I would ride that 350 back to Phoenix and on to California with two of my Nebraska friends, Mike Newlun and Brian Franzen. You can read that story, a great one, in *Southwest by Two-Stroke: Riding 350 Yamahas to California* (Rogue Phoenix Press, 2019).

Appendix A

Destinations, Highways, and Overnight Stays During Our Trip
This is the general overview. Some minor highways and brief
side trips are not listed.

First Leg: Larry and Jim Ride from Casa Grande, Arizona to York, Nebraska
Casa Grande Arizona to Phoenix Arizona I-10
Phoenix, Arizona to Flagstaff, Arizona I-17
Flagstaff, Arizona to Durango, Colorado Highway 89 to Highway 160
(Camped out in a field east of Durango)
Durango, Colorado to Stirling, Colorado Highway 160 to I-25 to Highway 6
(Camped out on picnic tables).
Stirling, Colorado to York, Nebraska
Highway 6 to Highway 81
(Stayed a few days at Jeff's house in York—beds and a shower)

Second Leg: Larry, Jeff, and Jim ride from York, Nebraska to Winnipeg, Manitoba to Yellowstone, Wyoming to Provo, Utah to Phoenix/Casa Grande, Arizona
York, Nebraska to Watertown, South Dakota Highway 81
(Motel room due to heavy rain)
Watertown, South Dakota to Grafton, North Dakota Highway 81

(Camped out two nights in construction yard)
Grafton, North Dakota to Winnipeg, Manitoba Highway 81 to Manitoba 75
Winnipeg, Manitoba to Weyburn, Saskatchewan Manitoba 2
(Spent the night in abandoned house somewhere between Winnipeg, Manitoba and Weyburn, Saskatchewan—howling rainstorm)
Weyburn, Saskatchewan to Plentywood, Montana Highway Saskatchewan 35 to US 85 to Highway 5
Plentywood, Montana to Miles City, Montana Highway 16 to I-94
(Camped out at rest area under picnic tables—Thunderstorm and spiders)
Miles City, Montana to Billings, Montana I-94
Billings, Montana to Yellowstone Park, Wyoming Highway 212
(Camped in Yellowstone Park in "No Camping" area)
Yellowstone, Wyoming to Provo, Utah Highway 191 to Highway 89 to I80
(Stayed in motel room and Jim installed a new tire)
Provo, Utah to Page, Arizona Highway 89
(Camped out in the desert under crackling power lines)
Page, Arizona to Flagstaff, Arizona Highway 89 to I-40
Flagstaff, Arizona to Phoenix, Arizona I-17
(Trip basically ends for Larry and Jim. They would continue down the I-10 from Phoenix to Casa Grande Area. Jeff stays a few days with his grandparents and aunt and uncle in Phoenix area)

Third Leg: Jeff rides from Phoenix, Arizona to York, Nebraska.
Tempe, Arizona to Vaughn, New Mexico Highway 60
(Motel Room in Vaughn, New Mexico)
Vaughn, New Mexico to Dalhart, Texas 54
(Motel Room in Dalhart, Texas … met his dad on open road the next day)
Dalhart, Texas to Kingman, Kansas Highway 54
Kingman, Kansas to Aurora, Nebraska Highway 14
Aurora, Nebraska to York, Nebraska Highway 34
(Home. Trip concludes)

Other Motorcycle Adventures

Riding Across New Mexico and Texas: Two Adventures
By Jim Balding

Many of the motorcycle stories in this book mention rain. Here's another one... with a tarantula twist.

In the late 70s, I decided to ride my Water Buffalo 750 from Arizona to Oklahoma City to visit my aunt. I headed down through Tucson on I-10 and rolled across New Mexico on the same freeway. The weather was so d*** hot I didn't even bother to take a jacket or sweatshirt or anything. The temps were blazing hot in Arizona and super-hot in New Mexico.

I turned northward at Las Cruces on Highway 70 and started climbing into the mountains after Alamogordo. Near forested Ruidoso, which is famous for horse racing, the clouds thickened and the rain started. I mean the heavens opened up and I was soaked and chilled. My teeth were actually chattering I was so cold, even though an hour or so earlier I had been burning up. I finally got down off the mountain and the terrain sort of flattened out. I pulled over and warmed my hands over the engine block of my motorcycle. I was still really cold. But the rain was following me. The rain started again like crazy and the desert on both sides of Highway 70 was filled with water... huge lakes and ponds everywhere.

Then, somewhere between Hondo and Roswell, New Mexico,

suddenly, I saw "them." The scene was from a *Svengoolie* movie. Tarantulas were being flooded out of their desert burrows and were running around on the highway! Some of those things were at least eight inches across. Big and ugly. Hairy, desperate spiders were everywhere. They were like rats or mice or squirrels! I was doing my best to dodge the scurrying creatures, but most cars I saw simply couldn't avoid the spiders and ran over and squished the poor arachnids. Gruesome brown and black blotches and body parts and legs could be seen everywhere on the road. I was on a miserable highway of death! I finally got out of there and away from the highway of spider destruction.

Later, I was hauling a** on I-40 somewhere in Texas between Amarillo and the Oklahoma border. Tucked in over the tank, I was rolling along at about 100 mph, making up for lost "rain and spider" time. I was going through a stretch of gentle rolling hills. Suddenly, at the top of a rise, I saw a patrol car facing me in the distance. Crap. I rolled off the throttle. Before long, lights flashing, the officer had me pulled over.

Wearing sunglasses and a "smokey" hat, he walked around me and the bike and said... "I'll be d***! That motorcycle has a radiator. S**********, boy, you were puttin' er down out on the 40. Well, even though I clocked you at 102, I'm just going to write you up for doing 90 seeing how you are a visitor here in Texas. You can pay the fine in the next town at the address listed right there on the ticket. Boy, you have a nice day.... And slow that S********** down." He walked back to his patrol car mumbling about motorcycles and radiators. I could swear I saw him step on a tarantula before he got back to the car! I was always careful going through Texas after that. S***********!

A Tarantula

My 1977 Ride from Arizona to Nebraska on an RD 250
By Jeffrey Ross

After attending Arizona State University in the spring of 1977, I decided to finish my studies at the University of Nebraska in Lincoln. The reasons for my decision are now forgotten, but that's what I did. I drove my car (with belongings and a Siamese cat named Winchester) back to Nebraska in early summer to get myself situated and to prepare for school in the fall. But after a week or two, I realized I missed my desert-bound 1973 blue and white Yamaha RD 250.

Getting ready to leave Casa Grande for Nebraska on my RD 250

I took a Continental Bus back to Casa Grande Arizona, did a little light maintenance work on the bike, and embarked on the 1200-mile return trip to the Midwest. (I took the same basic route described above in the *Two-Strokes to Canada* story above. In fact, I have probably been on that Highway 60-54 pathway 20-30 times in or on different vehicles during my lifetime.) My dad, Doyle Ross, rode the first 200 miles with me on his Vetter-fairing equipped Suzuki Titan (500cc twin). He went as far as Springerville, Arizona and then returned home the same day.

My Dad ready to ride out from Casa Grande on his Suzuki Titan

I took only two-lane highways—first dicing through the canyons and mountains, then rolling hundreds of miles through broad, high foothills and prairies, and finally coasting into the warm humid air of cornfields and my new university home.

I made the trip in two and one-half days. I spent the first night in a motel room in Vaughn, New Mexico, the second night under a picnic table in a park near Liberal, Kansas (as a vicious lightning and hailstorm pounded away. Yes, another picnic table. But no spiders this time). I easily arrived back in Lincoln, Nebraska before sunset on the third day. The RD ran perfectly—turbine smooth. I rolled along between 65-75 mph effortlessly, even pushing the large wind screen I borrowed from my dad. I replenished the Autolube daily, oiled the chain after each rainstorm, and achieved about forty-five mpg. That was long before smart phones, earplugs, GPS, and sound systems. I just loved the ride.

The drum brake-equipped RD was a strong running 250. It would out accelerate a friend's 1972 piston port Yamaha 350 R5C (with the black and orange paint scheme) up to about eighty mph. With sadness, I had to sell that long-distance 250 the next year to help pay for tuition.

At the time, I thought nothing of riding such a small machine cross-country. I just rolled along, embracing the open road, freedom, and enjoying the continuous howl of that beautiful two-stroke. Yes, I would probably do it again today.

Riding the Arizona Rim Road with My Folks
by Jeffrey Ross

On a Sunday morning back in November 2010, I rode one of my motorcycles (a 2004 Harley Sportster 883) from my home in Gilbert, Arizona, to Payson, Arizona, a ride of about eighty-seven miles, where my parents (Doyle and Pat Ross) lived.

My dad and mom, in their sidecar rig, then rode with me over to St. Johns, Arizona, to the Big Steel Cottage (a domesticated Quonset hut I still use for a "getaway"). We spent the night and came back to Payson later on Monday afternoon. The distance from Payson to St. Johns is roughly 135 miles one way. About half of the trip is over Highway 260, also known as the Rim Road here in Arizona. That part of the ride is always very pretty: Ponderosa pines, open meadows, forest cabins, and scenic vistas. Much of the elevation is over 7000 feet. The weather was very nice that late fall afternoon, mid-sixties, though temps were down to about freezing at night (The building has a propane wall heater and we stayed quite warm).

My parents' sidecar rig was a 2000 Ural 650. Interesting enough, that was the second time they had owned that particular motorcycle. My dad sold the rig to a fellow down in Tucson back in 2006. He then bought it back from him in the summer of 2010 after seeing it advertised on Craigslist. That brings us to the most interesting "sidebar" to this story.

You see, in February 2009, at age eighty-two, my dad fell on some ice in his driveway and badly broke his leg. He had to have surgery and underwent a long, at times perilous, recovery. After the hospital stay, he was in an assisted-care facility for a time, then wheelchair bound for weeks. He eventually graduated to a walker in early summer. He thought his motorcycle riding days might be over. But by mid-July, he was walking, helped by a cane, with vigor. He started thinking about bikes again. Then he found his old sidecar rig.

And that is why our Rim Road ride that fall was so special. He returned to the road.

At eighty-two, he was back on the highway. Certainly, he has had a long love affair with our sport. His first bike, at age seventeen in 1944, was a 1940 H-D 45. Dad's membership with the American Motorcycle Association originally began in the late forties. He and his brother Valta, and their dad, SE Ross, had an Indian dealership in Aurora, Nebraska during the late forties and early fifties.

Of course, his love of motorcycles is only surpassed by his love for my mom, Pat Ross. And she rode behind him (or next to him) or alongside him (on her own Kawasaki 250 single for a while) for over sixty years.

He finally decided to stop riding motorcycles at age ninety. It was his decision. Now, at nearly ninety-three, he is still very interested in "cool" machinery. Just a short time ago, in March 2020, he purchased a very nice 1949 Studebaker Champion so he and my mom can still cruise in style.

Thoughts on my 2004 Harley Sportster 883
by Jeffrey Ross

My decision to buy a new Harley-Davidson Sportster, back in the fall of 2004, was made with great emotional trepidation. I have been riding bikes since 1969, mostly on the street and entirely Japanese (except for one old NSU Fox we recovered from a barn in Nebraska). I must tell you; I miss two-strokes so much. I had some great ones, including Yamaha R2s, R5s, RDs, Kawasaki H-1s, Avengers, Water Buffalos— far too many to recount. I should have kept them all.

I watched that whole Harley phenomena develop in the late nineties and two thousands. You know, the Dyna Glide as "social furniture" metaphor. Of course, we still see thousands of sharp looking Harleys every day, rumbling down the road, parked at chic watering holes, herded together at restaurants, blue engine night lights flashing, and gregariously befitted with more Screamin' Eagle accessories than rapper Santa Claus could provide in a millennium.

I bought one of the new rubber-mounted Sportsters back in 2004, a rather handsome silver XL 883 standard. My aforementioned dilemma about buying the Sporty had nothing to do with the 883 vs. 1200 debate (or about what aftermarket parts to buy. I kept my Sporty pretty much original except for some V&H mufflers, a passenger seat, and a K&N air filter). Of course, I took a lot of flak from my Japanese and German bike riding friends about buying a Hawg. My dad, Doyle, had been an Indian and Vincent guy in the fifties. He thought it amusing I would purchase a

Harley of any kind.

The Sportster was a fun ride. No one can deny there is just something about that sound, the feel, and those handling characteristics which make the Sporty a fetching bike. Sure, it wasn't all that quick, but the bike provided an excellent ride for hundreds of miles at a time.

The 883's paint and chrome were excellent. The slip-on mufflers (with quiet baffles) really enhanced the magical V-twin sound. The bike tracked well, stopped sufficiently, and managed around fifty mpg. And being a "Harley," the bike naturally drew that "celebrity" attention at gas stations. I had always dreamed (long before reaching aged maturity) of buying an 883. But when the Motor Company rubber mounted the engine, and the magazine reviews came out positive, I knew the time had come to go Harley.

What is my conundrum, my problem, my concern? It was (and remains) not really psychological. The difficulty, the struggle, with my decision to buy and continue to ride a Hawg is sociological, or more accurately, cultural. Here is the crux of the matter: I didn't feel like I fit in with 21st century observable main-stream Harley culture.

Oh, I watched *American Thunder* once in a while, but I have no desire to be part of the Sturgis Crowd. I owned one or two H-D T-shirts, but there were no expensive Motor Clothes in my closet or on my wish list. I don't ever ride with a group of more than three (usually I go riding solo or with my son or dad).

You'd never see a beautiful curvy woman, wearing chaps or a leather tube top, riding with me or shopping with me in tow at an H-D store. I'm just a guy who appreciates the history and technological evolution (however glacial), of the Motor Company's two wheeled products... and their sound. Here is what it comes down to:

My sense of "Harley" doesn't really match up with America's current corporate glossy perceptions of Motor Company ethos. Two themes dominate my mental images of what constitutes "Harley-ness." One theme is colored orange and black—Harley Davidson Racing— especially dirt track racing. C'mon—Bart Markel... Dick Mann... Scott

Parker... Jennifer Snyder. What's better? I love Moto GP, but there is just something about flat tracking that is hard to beat. I have so much respect and admiration for one of my closest friends, Frank Westerman, who raced a KR 750 on Albuquerque tracks (Coronado and Speedway Park), in Texas, and in Kansas back in the sixties.

The other theme has its roots in my formative teenage years. My favorite TV show of all time is *Then Came Bronson*, starring Michael Parks, about the solitary guy headed nowhere and yet everywhere on a sixties-era Sportster. He wore a blue stocking cap, some gnarly old denim clothes, probably smelled like oil, and had a duffle bag strapped to the handlebars or his headlight and some other bag as passenger. Oh, there were a few lovely girls scattered around in the episodes, but they certainly didn't see his spark plug fouling XLH as a fashion statement or badge of wealth. He was fed up with the system and rode out.

That may have been the best part of the show. He rode *out*, not down to the Bike Night at Hooters. That image of a solitary Bronson, riding across the cold (or hot) California desert, is fixed forever in my still (to this day) developing mind. My conceptual frame of what a Sporty rider should be like is (still) solitary and strong, and distant.

I guess that's my struggle. I'm not asocial. I'm just not social (or socially motivated) in the Harley culture sense. (I know for sure I'm not a racer!) When I visited the Hawg shop for a part or oil, I always found the staff courteous, helpful, and professional. Very nice people. But I wasn't comfortable.

Perhaps I'm a little too rough around the edges, a bit too blue around the collar for their world. I may have too much misplaced class sensitivity or a kind of misdirected experiential motorcycle arrogance. I know I don't fantasize about things I will never have or need. Nonetheless, I just got up and rode and came home happy. Oh well. I loved my Sporty. Love your Harley if you ride one. Cool machinery. Very cool.

Jeff's 2004 Sportster

Jim and Les Ride from Arizona to Oregon in 1974 on Suzuki Two-Strokes

By Jim Balding

Jim and Les Just before leaving on their 1974 trip.

Occasionally, two or three or four events during a motorcycle ride are really memorable. Back in 1974, Les Black (one of our great friends from Casa Grande) and I took a ride up through California to Oregon. I rode my GT 750 Suzuki triple, and he took his Suzuki GT 550 triple. We left Casa Grande and headed up to Phoenix and found our way to Highway 93… the main drag up to Las Vegas. After spending a day or two seeing the lights and fooling around in Vegas, we rolled over to

Ontario, California to spend some time with my relatives (who owned a go kart track). We also stopped off in Sacrament briefly to visit with a couple of girls Les knew. After that, we veered over to the PCH (Pacific Coast Highway). Our general plan was to motor toward San Francisco and check out the big attractions like Alcatraz and the Golden Gate Bridge.

Well, somehow around the Golden Gate Park, we became separated on the freeways. I pulled over alongside the road and tried to figure out where I was. A very pleasant motorcycle cop on a Moto Guzzi pulled over to see if I needed help. I explained to him what happened, and I told him I was a bit lost. Before he resumed his patrol, he kindly gave me good directions to the Pinole Hercules community where Les and I had originally planned to spend the night. (The area was much smaller back then and had only one motel.) But there I was, all alone and no Les. I rode along solo for a few more miles and finally entered Pinole, and then I checked into the motel and thought of a way to get ahold of Les. Remember, this was 1974.

I found a pay phone and called my mom back in Arizona. I asked her to call Les' house in Casa Grande and tell them where I was, hoping he would call there sometime that afternoon or evening to check in and learn of my whereabouts. My plan worked. I went back inside the motel and cleaned up. About three hours later, I heard that distinct GT 550 sound outside the room. Les had found the motel. Cell phones would have been easier, but we connected regardless. That was our only separation event on the trip.

Our original idea was to spend a few days in Frisco and then return home. But Les got some kind of news from home that encouraged him to want to stay out on the ride a little longer. We decided to head up into Oregon and visit Portland. We didn't make it quite that far, but we did have a couple of adventures in southern Oregon before returning back.

Somewhere in Oregon— I don't remember the exact city— we ended up going the wrong-way on a one-way road and got pulled over by a policeman. We gave him our sad story about being from Arizona and not knowing what we were doing. I guess he felt sorry for us and let us go. We decided to get a beer or two to celebrate or commiserate and have some dinner before finding a place to camp for the evening. We ended in an underground bar. I remember the air smelled like skunk p*** as we headed down the sloping sidewalk into the establishment. Once our eyes adjusted, we found a place to sit and tried to order a pitcher of Coors beer. Well, the server said, "Sorry, we don't have any Coors beer." He told us the local beer of choice was Pabst Blue Ribbon. What's that saying: "When in Rome, do what the Romans do"? Surprised, but very thirsty, we ordered up a pitcher. Tasted great. Smelled funny....

While we were enjoying our pitcher, we met a couple of really cute girls who invited us to a gathering nearby. They gave us directions and assured us they would see us at the party. So later, after we ate something, we thought we would go to the party. Les had carefully written down the instructions, but we ended up, on our motorcycles, at sort of a dead end on a river. We thought we had been played by those girls. You might say we were not happy. Tired from the day's ups and downs, we decided to camp out in a nice spot near that river. The next morning, we noticed a steel bridge over the water not too far away. We found our way to the bridge by back tracking a little and discovered it was the same street! Just in a different place. Crazy. Had we known, we would have easily made it to the party and had a few more beers and met up with those cute girls. They weren't fooling with us after all. Darn it. Thinking back, maybe they thought we brushed them off.

Here's one more interesting tidbit from Oregon. We stopped some place to eat Mexican food. I ordered up a plate of beef taquitos. The server brought me some hot dogs in rolled tortillas! Didn't seem right to me.

On our way back, we more or less blasted down I-5 and headed south. We spent some time in Weed, California at a pizza place and headed over to Susanville on Highway 89/44. This is beautiful country near Mount Shasta and the Lassen Volcanic Park. But I remember getting just pelted by rain and hail. Now getting all wet was one thing, but that intense rainstorm evidently splashed up some slime or fungus or something off the roadway that gave me a terrible rash. Les didn't have the same problem, but I broke out all over in a bad rash right after that rainstorm. We came back through that part of northern California without much incident.

Later, we cruised through Reno, Nevada and then had a most interesting side trip. We came to a place south and east of Reno where we could see an older version of the highway, or some kind of paved road, all blocked off by barricades, kind of veering off. The old road clearly stretched off into the distance, into the mountains. The road looked pretty good except for all the weeds growing up through the cracks and holes. Anyway, we decided to see where the unused road went. Les and I found a way around the barricades and rolled down that deserted pavement for a couple of hours, through lovely mountains and hills. To our good fortune, the derelict road met up with Highway 95.

After leaving Reno and dipping back into California, one of the highlights was going around Death Valley and Devil's Hole on Highway 95. This was the summertime and quite warm, you know, so we didn't enter the Valley itself. And that intense heat down there was making my newly acquired road slime rash really uncomfortable. I was itching a lot. The heat made the situation almost unbearable.

The trip was about over. Re-entering Nevada on Highway 95,

we spent a couple of days again in Vegas, probably hanging in clubs or casinos. Here is a great story from our return to the Vegas community. We were at one of those exotic dancer places and they were having amateur night. All these guys and their girlfriends and wives were there—some of the ladies would go up and dance with or without clothes. Everybody was having a great time. Les and I had front row seats for some reason. Les, the poor guy, was so worn out from the trip he was nearly dozing off despite the music and action.

One of the dancers, during her "act," saw Les was falling asleep. She came over and sat on the stage and wrapped her ankles around his neck. "Hey, you can't fall asleep during my act," she angrily shouted. Les, startled, hollered, "Oh no, oh no, I'm not asleep!" The place erupted in laughter and shouting. Funnier than h***! I think the story even made it down to Casa Grande later.

After all the excitement and fun, we found our way to Arizona and made it back to Casa Grande and reality. Good trip.

A Kawasaki Sidewinder and Mach III Go Fishing
By Michael Newlun

My dad, Tom Newlun, is an accomplished mechanic. From the age of seven, I grew up watching over his shoulder, sometimes holding the light as he worked. I learned to take care of my bicycle and fix my own flats.

When I turned sixteen, I was already on my third car, a genuine muscle car. A 1964 Plymouth Sport Fury 383 4-speed. Later, and I don't remember what car I had at the time, I had also already owned and sold a Kawasaki motorcycle. Of course, I wanted another one. In the spring of 1972, I found a Kawasaki 238 dirt bike called a Sidewinder. The machine had been stripped down somewhat and used for racing. I was advised not to buy the Kawasaki, so, of course, I did anyway. That's what I did and what I still do.

I discovered the voltage regulator didn't regulate, or it was missing completely. I'm not sure which. I do know the one time I tried to come home from out of town after dark, I revved up the engine and the headlight lamp blew out. To make it safely home, I had to follow a car and rode close behind, almost on their bumper, so that I could see the road. Crazy!

After I did a little mechanical and electrical work and got the Sidewinder running pretty well, one April weekend I rode from Aurora to York, Nebraska to pick up my buddy, Jeff Ross, and go on an overnight camping and fishing trip. Jeff was all packed up and ready to go, so we quickly hit the highway on our adventure. We rode our motorcycles about thirty miles to my grandpa's sand pit (lake) he leased in Hordville, Nebraska. The small lake was right next to a bible camp called Covenant Cedars.

Jeff and I grew up camping or sleeping out every other night when we were kids. Now that we both liked to ride motorcycles, we just combined the two things we enjoyed and added fishing. The spring weather was great. Everything went smoothly. Jeff and I arrived at the lake without incident and set up camp, including my pup tent. Both of us fished for bass and caught enough for a nice supper and even released a few. Life was good. I fried up a batch of the fillets that were seasoned with a mix from my other friend's dad who sold Henny Penny Chicken seasonings and frying equipment. (The seasoning worked great on fish, too.)

Like Huck Finn and Tom Sawyer, we ate our fill by the water and buried the bones and other remains of the fish after supper, did what kids do, talked about motorcycles for a while, and then called it a night. Sometime later, just past midnight, a major thunderstorm rumbled through and we woke up to a downpour. Water had come in the front flap and pooled in the tent, completely soaking our clothes and gear. After the deluge, we didn't get much sleep, but we managed to get in a few winks.

The next morning, we were finally sleeping soundly when we were roused out of our slumber by a loud voice shouting, "Kids, kids, and motorcycles!" He didn't sound happy. He wasn't. After a few pensive moments, I managed to stick my head out and quickly notified the gentleman of who we were and who my grandpa was. I assured him everything was okay. We weren't hoods or bums or hippies. I recognized him immediately. He was a friend of my grandpa's, the man who shared the lease for use of the lake. I guess we had never met, or else he had forgotten me. Things calmed down a little. He wasn't happy about the trash strewn about. At first, I couldn't figure out where the mess came from. I explained we had buried our garbage, but the racoons must have dug it up. I put on a humble face and apologized, and we cleaned up the debris. Things simmered down quickly, and everything seemed to be fine. We had a good time visiting with him about the beauty of the lake and excellent fishing. He left in an entirely different mood.

Later that day, Jeff and I packed up and headed home. We made our way to a little two-lane blacktop county road and headed east. As we were riding, I was deciding the little Sidewinder was actually okay. The Kawasaki was running great. Oh, the 238 had a lot of vibration from the knobby tires, but that was to be expected on pavement. Then, all of a sudden, I was looking down at the headlight and thinking, "Boy, the brakes sure work good." But I wasn't on the brakes. I had not touched them. I grabbed the clutch and the bike shot back under me. I had a sick feeling. I let out the clutch lever and I knew what had happened when the back wheel just skidded under me. Piston seizure: the engine was frozen since the piston had welded itself to the cylinder. Not good. Fail!

I slowly rolled to the side of the road. The bike was done! We used the left-hand tow method to make it into this little town, and I mean little town, Polk, a few miles further. We found a tiny ice cream stand or something like that, but it wasn't part of the DQ chain. Jeff and I got a bite to eat and told the people running the establishment about our problem. We knew we couldn't make the trip all the way to York down Highway 81 using that flimsy and unsafe towing method. I asked the proprietors for permission to leave the bike out back behind the restaurant, and I promised to come back and pick it up in few days.

Nebraska people being sympathetic, they understood and agreed to look after the recently dead Sidewinder. Feeling somewhat better, I packed up my gear and we reshuffled Jeff's luggage and started out for York two-up on his 500. Riding passenger on that beautiful Mach III, I was immediately astounded by the smooth ride and amazing power. I felt like I was on a jet! I was in awe. But that just wasn't the end of our troubles. Before we could finish the brief ride home, heavy rain started again. We didn't have any rain gear with us, for some reason. Jeff and I were each wearing fashionable, for the time, jean jackets. Before long, we were soaked clear through.

Eventually, we stopped at a farmhouse along the west side of Highway 81. The place had the typical covered wrap-around porch. I knocked on the door, and the little old lady who answered gave us permission to stand out of the rain till it "let up a little." I don't blame her for not welcoming us in. We looked like two drowned rats. I can't recollect how long we waited, but we eventually mounted up and went to Jeff's house without further problems. I don't remember how I got back home to Aurora, but if I were guessing, I'll bet I was a passenger in Jeff's black 1959 Rambler station wagon (with the three on the tree and overdrive transmission and "holey" floorboard).

I had to tell Dad what happened and, of course, I got a lecture for buying that motorcycle in the first place. We took the shop pickup truck and picked up the Sidewinder and hauled it to a mechanic near Columbus who Dad had contacted to make the repairs. (This was at the same shop Jeff bought his Mach III the previous fall.)

When I picked up the bike back a few weeks later, I remember the mechanic telling me the Sidewinder was a really fast little bike. Sure was. But I sold it. I had ridden on a Mach III and I knew what I was missing.

Jim and Reymundo Ride Water Buffalos to Laguna Seca Raceway

By Jim Balding

Rey Castellano and I rode our Suzuki 750 triples (Water Buffalos) up to Monterrey, California in the summer of 1977 to watch motorcycles races. Rey rode over from Casa Grande, Arizona to Stanfield, Arizona where I was spending the weekend with my folks. We took I-8 and headed up Highway 85 to Buckeye, Arizona where we picked up I-10 and travelled west toward Indio and Palm Springs. Later, near San Bernadino, California, we took a cut off road toward Lancaster and bypassed Riverside and LA and all of the metro area. Rey and I eventually turned north on the 101 and stayed on that road all the way to near Monterrey where the Laguna Seca Raceway is located. The track was built back in the late fifties, is just over two miles in length, and has a peculiar downhill corkscrew which makes for exciting racing. We spent three days watching a big AMA motorcycle racing event. Some of the most famous names in bike racing of the time were competing: people like Kawasaki tuner Pops Yoshimura and Reg Pridmore on his blazing fast BMW.

**A modern photo of the Corkscrew...Notice tires have replaced
earlier hay bales
(Image courtesy *Wikipedia* Commons)**

We had a great time. Seems like thousands of motorcycles were parked everywhere in a large grassy area. Rey and I just threw out our sleeping bags next to our bikes for the whole time. Nobody seemed to be messing with anybody's gear. There were porta-potties but no showers. I remember we lived on expensive (for the era) vendor food and beer. Plenty of beer! We loved hearing the sounds of both street and racing motorcycles. People were everywhere. Sadly, the works Suzuki Team decided not to race at the event that year, which disappointed me. We were big Suzuki fans for sure.

Here are some highlights from the races. We thoroughly enjoyed watching the sidecar guys. Two gents on a highly modified Water Buffalo won their class. On the podium, one of the two-man team members said, "We are proud to represent Suzuki even though the factory teams decided not to compete!" Sort of made my day to see those privateers succeed on a Suzuki.

Rey and I watched most of the races from the bottom of the Corkscrew. During one event, some racer took a front-end dive going downhill and crashed into the hay bales protecting spectators, who were standing around everywhere! Such a thing would not be allowed in 2021. Hay bales and motorcycle pieces went flying and tumbling all over the place. A few minutes later, the media showed up with cameras and microphones and all that. Somebody asked the crashed rider how he felt. He hollered out, "I busted my n***! I busted my n***! Ahhrrr!" Anyway, they hauled the poor guy off to the medic tent to check on him. His bike was pretty much destroyed.

The event had some kind of an amateur race where you could get out there on your bike and race in an open class (any size machine) as long as the motorcycle passed an inspection. That meant safety wiring and taping everything which could break or cause trouble on the track. We saw a guy on a Yamaha 400 competing with bigger bikes. He could really haul through the corners but got passed on the straightaways. The dude was very patient, like you-know-who in the Tortoise and Hare story, and finished fourth.

That trip was a lot of fun and my only experience at Laguna Seca. Rey made quite a few trips over to the track. He really loved the ride and the area and the races. Here's something. We didn't have any rain or bad weather on that particular trip.

Coming home was uneventful, I'd say. Hot as always in southern California and Arizona. We came home much the same way we went up and bypassed LA. We got off I-10 at Indio, cruised past the Salton Sea, and went to El Centro where we picked up our old friend I-8. We went over to Yuma where I got off the freeway and headed south to Somerton. Rey went home to Casa Grande. Rey was one of our friends who really loved two-stroke motorcycles, especially Kawasakis and Suzukis. A great guy.

The Sweet Sixteen Honda CB 175
By Julie Sego

Julie Ross on her CB 175 in York Nebraska 1973.

As long as I can remember, my family has been obsessed with anything containing an engine: cars, boats, planes, and most importantly, motorcycles! That fascination has certainly passed on through generations. My grandfathers and uncles had motorcycles, and both my parents rode, so destiny seemingly required I would share this addictive love for biking.

My older brother, Jeff, obtained his license and, at age sixteen, received a brand-new bike, a high-pipe black and white 350cc Yamaha two-stroke. He was so proud. I was a little jealous, but I realized I had to wait my turn. For years, we were a family of four on two motorcycles: Mom and Dad on one bike and Jeff and I on the other. (Jeff used to do wheelies with me on back. I loved it, but our mom didn't.) I thought my brother was the coolest dude ever, and I wanted to follow in his footsteps.

Just a couple of years later, in 1973, I suppose unsurprisingly, the tradition continued for me when I received a brand-new red and black Honda CB 175 for my own sixteenth birthday. I recall having my birthday party in our basement in York, Nebraska. Interestingly enough, two of Jeff's friends from Arizona, Tim Allison and Jim Balding, were travelling on their motorcycles through Nebraska that day. Tim and Jim happened to stop by our house, and they ended up attending my party, too. Some of the presents I received included riding gloves, a can of Turtle Wax, and an assortment of bungee cords. Not a typical "Sweet 16" party or gifts! After years of driving go karts and riding a minibike and a Honda 50 in my youth, I felt like I finally hit the big leagues.

The Doyle Ross Motorcycle Training Institute

As with my brother, and later my mother, I was taught motorcycle riding by my dad—at what I like to call the "Doyle Ross Motorcycle Training Institute." (My dad was a phenomenal motorcyclist, having ridden since he was sixteen as did his father before him.)

With permit in hand, my months of rider training began on a dirt path track located next to Hurlbut Cycle Shop just north of York, Nebraska (where the bike was purchased) on Highway 81. Many evenings before dinner, we went to the track so I could practice riding... and practice was always a highlight of my day. Anyway, maneuvering a street bike in the dirt was challenging. We always had the track to ourselves, which helped with my nerves and concentration. My dad was strict but extremely practical as a teacher.

I recall one eventful session clearly. During laps, I came around a turn which had a slight upgrade before leveling off to a stop where Dad stood. Unfortunately, I stopped too quickly, and the bike started falling to the side. As I was losing my grip and yelling for my dad to help me, he stood there with his hands firmly on his waist. He didn't say a word. Mind you, I was barely ninety-five pounds and five feet tall, and even this smaller cc size bike was still massive compared to my frame. Well, as you probably guessed, the bike went completely over (fortunately the low muffler pipe didn't pin my leg or burn my jeans).

The bike lay silent on the track, and my hands still gripped the handlebars. I looked up at my dad, almost in tears of frustration. He continued just standing there, not making a sound. The silence was brutal. I mustered my strength and pulled the bike upright, then placed it on the side stand. I looked intently at my dad, puzzled. Why didn't he help his daughter? Finally, he spoke. Dad said, "I won't always be there to help you and you may be in a situation where no one else is around, so you'll just have to do it." Then, after a long pause, he spoke again. "Hopefully you learned from this today." I certainly knew if the situation was serious, he would not have let me get hurt. We didn't say much else, and soon thereafter, we went home.

I was mad at him for a while, but I also realized he was right. I had made an error by braking incorrectly, and I alone would have to remedy my skill deficiency. I know my dad was there to support me and prepare me to be a good motorcyclist and, in turn, just a better motorist all around. For that, I will always be grateful. The rest of my training went easier as the months followed, and I was thrilled to "graduate" from the Institute. I had dad's approval to go forward with obtaining my motorcycle license.

Motorcycle License Examination Day

As I noted earlier, I had ridden small displacement bikes as a kid, but everyone dreams of that magic day of turning 16 and officially becoming a legal motorcyclist. Mine was a hot, humid summer day in

1973. Dad and I rode my red and black 1972 Honda CB 175 motorcycle to the downtown York Nebraska testing location. He dropped me off and then walked to his workplace (a couple blocks away). He was an insurance salesman in York. I told him I'd be back when finished, and I'd take him home to get his car as planned. I was picturing this in my head already as I entered the license division in the basement of an old WPA-era building. I had been training with dad for months and had his approval to proceed. He felt confident I was ready, as did I.

As I approached the examiner's table with my red sparkly helmet in hand, I felt all eyes were upon me, mainly because I was young— and a girl. Everyone looked so surprised! I told the examiner I was there to get my motorcycle license. He said, "What? What are you talking about?" I presented all the formal paperwork and the fee payment, and he just shook his head. He kept asking if my parents were aware of what I was doing, if that was what I really wanted, like he just couldn't believe my intent and was trying to talk me out of it.

Getting a motorcycle license was a completely normal process within my family, no matter what gender, and this examiner was ruining my big day. He was making me a little angry, and my stress level was elevating rapidly! I was firm and politely held my ground. He finally was accepting of the fact, although I can still remember the snickering and puzzled facial expressions from the other people in the room. Mr. Examiner finally realized I was serious. I took the written examination and passed. I don't recall the grade. But I was very happy; step one was completed. I had one final step to go on my journey.

We headed outdoors and I led him to where my bike was parked. I told him I had arrived with my dad and would pick him up at work after the test. He said it was a nice-looking bike. I told him it was my birthday present from my parents. He was shocked again! Anyway, he continued with questions and wanted proof of ownership and insurance. I still felt like, as a young girl, I was having to prove myself. After complying with all his requirements, it was time. I was nervous, of course, but anxious to begin. My instructions were to cover the city blocks in a figure eight pattern TWICE. The majority of the turns would be out of his view (yay!) except the starting/stopping point and for one block in each direction. Piece of cake, I thought.

As I maneuvered the streets, I tried to keep calm and concentrate. The first pass went great. The ride felt so natural, and I was relieved the license was almost in my grasp. Just the second pass to go. As I signaled a right turn, I slowed down and then stopped at the corner stop sign and checked the traffic. Then, disaster. Moving forward from the stop, I failed to give the Honda enough gas, slipped the clutch, and killed the engine. This happened to be the corner where the examiner stood. And to top it off, my dad (who was only a few blocks away) was standing outside on the corner! He had seen my mishap as well. My heart sank. I was so embarrassed and so mad at myself. I looked over as the examiner wrote something on his clipboard and said, "We're done." I wanted to go again immediately to prove myself. I was disappointed, yes, but it was certainly a learning moment that day. I had to wait an entire week to try again. That was the rule. The next week, my second attempt, I passed. I was so elated! I just knew I could get my motorcycle license.

Immediately after getting my license that day, I went home, grabbed a quick bite, and told my mom I was riding over to Waco, Nebraska. (About a fifteen minute trip down busy Highway 34. I hadn't been on that road before.) Aghast, she exclaimed, "You can't do that alone. You just got your license this morning!" She was worried for me, of course, but I wanted to hit the open pavement for real. I rode to Waco, about ten miles away, parked under a shade tree, and never left my bike seat. I rested a bit, did some reflecting, and then motored home (although I really wanted to keep going!). I think I was only gone a half hour to forty-five minutes. I felt so grown up, like I'd driven hundreds of miles. It was the best day and best feeling ever. I was finally official and so happy and proud. Another generation had begun riding.

Riding "Little Toot"

By Patricia Ross

I rode as a passenger behind my husband, Doyle, for many years, starting in the late 1940s. He had Indians, BMWs, Ducatis, Hondas, Kawasakis, and Suzukis, and I happily rode with him on all those machines. Then, in 1981 when I was about fifty, I realized I wanted my own motorcycle. I enjoyed riding with Doyle, but I wanted to personally experience that freedom of the open road, the two-lane highway, as a solo rider. Doyle was very supportive. We were living in an A-Frame house just north of Casa Grande, Arizona at the time. Doyle and I looked at several dealerships in town and even in Phoenix, but I couldn't find a motorcycle which felt right and also allowed me to touch the ground comfortably with both feet. Well, we went to Australia for the month of July that summer to celebrate our anniversary. Doyle still likes to say we had no July 4th that year because we were Down Under.

Right after we came home, the Kawasaki dealer in Casa Grande called and said he had the perfect motorcycle for me: a brand-new blue CSR 250 four-stroke single. We went down to the shop immediately. I would say it was love at first sight and a perfect fit. After a brief price negotiation with the dealer, we bought the machine that I lovingly came to call "Little Toot." Doyle rode the 250 the ten miles or so home after it was prepped and ready. A day or two passed, and then he said it was time for me to learn to ride. For about a half hour, he explained how the controls worked, described things to look out for, and reviewed situations

76

to consider. Then we rolled Little Toot across the dirt road in front of our house and out into a big field filled mostly with Creosote bushes and a few cacti.

He taught me how to ride using the same formula he used to teach our son, Jeff and daughter, Julie. I sat on the machine and started it up with the kick starter. I was nervous. Then he said, "You're gonna ride it. Stay on it and get going or get off." So, I killed the engine a time or two but finally started rolling forward in first gear. He walked briskly next to me, reminding me how to shift, accelerate, and brake. I didn't fall over, and I didn't hit any bushes. He told me, "If you fall over, you're gonna pick it up!" I never did drop my new motorcycle. After a couple of episodes like this, I was practicing frequently and before long was able to get out on the road and move through traffic without a problem. I guess I learned from the Doyle Ross "tough love learning to ride a motorcycle" treatment. But I remember clearly, he wasn't very "clingy" when I let out the clutch and gave it the gas the first time. He wanted me to succeed on my own, and his method worked.

During the early eighties, I was employed as the Special Education Department Secretary for the Sacaton School District in Pinal County. I rode the 250 over to my workplace many times. Sacaton was about twenty miles to the west of our home. To get there, I would take I-10 for about 10 miles and then turn off on the northbound Highway 187 and go a few miles before turning west again and eventually heading into Sacaton on a nice paved road. I rode that 250 at 65 mph down I-10 without any trouble.

I have two interesting memories from my Sacaton trips. I did have an almost embarrassing event. This happened not long after I began riding to my job. One afternoon, after work, I had just left the school. I guess I was about a mile out of town when the bike sputtered, slowed, and quit. I rolled off onto the shoulder, dismounted, and stood there looking at my paused Kawasaki. Things seemed very quiet, very still. There was no one around to help me. So, I sat there, thinking, and evaluating. Remember I told you that Doyle had discussed situations? I realized what happened after thinking a minute or two. Little Toot was out of gas! Or almost, anyway. I turned the gas valve, the petcock, to the reserve setting, started up the bike, and rode back into Sacaton to a service station and filled up Little Toot's blue gas tank. Then, I confidently rode on home. No problem. I was quite proud of myself for remembering what to do.

By the way, the kids at Sacaton Elementary were always asking me to take them for rides. I told them my insurance wouldn't cover passengers on the motorcycle. Since they were young, they didn't argue too much. But they asked me all the time. Nearly every day. I think they were fascinated by a lady riding around on a motorcycle.

Once I rode Little Toot over to Coolidge, a few miles away to the east, to check out a community yard sale. I couldn't have carried much home on my motorcycle, but I thought I would go see what was available. That was a fun day. On my way home, four gentlemen on Harley Baggers gave me an escort. We rode in an H pattern for a few miles before they waved and turned off.

Doyle and I took a few trips together, also. We would ride into Casa Grande to get breakfast on the weekends or take leisurely rides through the nearby farms and farming communities. One day, we decided to ride the seventy-five miles or so up Highway 60 to see our friends, George and Freda English, in San Carlos, Arizona. George was the shop teacher at the local high school. On our way back, near the Queen Creek Tunnel, we got caught in a big rainstorm and had to stop until the deluge quit. I will never forget that 150-mile round trip.

I rode Little Toot until the mid-eighties when Doyle retired. I'm not sure why I sold the bike at the time, but I remember a lady at the hospital where Doyle worked bought the machine from me. Little Toot was a good friend, and I have enjoyed sharing a few adventures with you.

**Early 1980s: Pat Ross and her brother Harry "Happy"
Reynolds check out Little Toot.**

My Journey with Motorcycles
By Terry Baugher

In 1970, while I was growing up in Michigan, my grandfather purchased a 1970 60cc Yamaha mini Enduro. That little 60cc motorcycle allowed my three younger brothers and me to learn how to ride bikes. Only one of us didn't continue riding later in life.

Our Yamaha Mini-Enduro

Over the course of the next year or two, as I outgrew the little Yamaha, I started wishing I had a road bike. In 1973, I was a junior in high school, and I was working as a short order cook in one of the local restaurants. That's where I had an opportunity to meet people who were heavily involved in motorcycling. The restaurant was one of those places where a customer sat at the counter and watched the person cook food on the other side—and customers could even talk to the cook.

At some point, I mentioned to a couple of people who were regulars that I wanted a motorcycle. One of those individuals was named Frenchy. He was the president of a local motorcycle club from Detroit called the Renegades. (Frenchy sadly died in 1994. He was instrumental in the next phase of my motorcycle journey.) One day, Frenchy made the comment he knew somebody who had a small street bike, a 1971 CB 350 Honda, which needed a little work. Frenchy thought the owner was willing to let it go for $400.

I drove over and looked at the motorcycle and found out it had been re-built into a drag bike meant just for racing at the track. On a positive note, the Honda came with boxes of original parts in various forms of disrepair. I ended up buying that 350. Then, I nursed the Honda back to life for the street. I removed the drag bars and replaced them with eight bend pull-back handlebars. Next, I put the stock seat back on and repaired and painted the gas tank. I had to install new tires and attach the fenders, lights, and gauges. Then, I put a tall sissy bar and pad on the back.

I noticed the engine didn't have any air cleaners. The racing carburetors were oversized and fitted with velocity stacks. I installed "net socks" to keep the bugs and dust from getting sucked into the carbs. The extant exhaust system ended at the front pegs and had no baffling. To fix the noise problem, I bought two little can opener baffles that could be shoved in the end, and I added a couple of screws to hold them and solve the decibel problem.

The bike was scary fast but street legal once again. A big issue was that, with a passenger, the front end wanted to come up in first, second, and third gear when I shifted. At night, when I "got on it" and revved the engine, flames about eight to ten inches long would come out of the exhaust pipes! But I was now on the road.

The following year, I was a senior in high school. The CB 350 was my daily driver except during rainstorms or in the middle of winter. At that time, I also had a 1967 Camaro that was my rainy-day or snow-day option—and a great time!

The CB 350 Former Dragster Restored to Street Form.

I eventually left the job at the restaurant and started working a variety of part-time jobs. One of those jobs was cooking burgers for the Burger Chef restaurant where I met my wife-to-be, Robin. Our first date was a motorcycle trip with a couple of other friends, out toward Pontiac, Michigan, on a long winding road. We got off work at 1:30 am and headed out. (I probably would've never asked her out, but since I had a way-cool motorcycle, she asked me and that was the start of our lifelong relationship.)

I took her home to her grandmother's house at 6 am. You know that didn't go over well. Two weeks later, Granny (who was raising Robin at the time) found out I had a motorcycle. During those two weeks I had shown up in my Camaro only—no Honda. The first dry day I came back on the Honda to pick up Robin for a ride, Granny hollered, "You're not getting on the back of that motorcycle, young lady!" Needless to say,

Robin did anyway, and we pulled out of the driveway and took off with the front tire in the air for the first three gears!

Our First Big Road Trip

Our initial big road trip occurred in 1975. We were now married, and Robin was six months pregnant with our first child. We had some friends at the time who, like us, were apartment managers. The four of us were running an apartment complex. We were on call for a week at a time each month. That allowed only one week a month when none of us were working. We finally found a time we could take a trip together.

John and his brother Jerry invited us to go on a ride with about a dozen other people. We were going to travel from the Detroit area westward across the state to the Sand Dunes on the shores of Lake Michigan near Muskegon. Robin agreed to go, even though she was six months "along." So far, during the time we had been together, she had never taken more than an hour to an hour and a half ride. But she was enthusiastic about seeing the Dunes, so we loaded up all of our stuff and headed out with the group. Rob and I were riding the smallest bike in the pack. They were shocked I had no problems keeping up.

John and Jerry were the pranksters of the group. At one point, while traveling down the road on the highway, Jerry was out front of the group, and he acted like something was wrong with his motorcycle. The next place we could pull off appeared to be a truck weigh station. As we all pulled into the exit ramp, I could see him looking back, and, as soon as everyone was committed and off the highway, he just took off. Funny guy. There were no trucks in the weigh station, so here we were, blasting across the scales, a dozen motorcycles just blowing through the facility at 70 mph trying to catch back up to Jerry. You could see people inside the buildings just staring as we flew by, got back on the highway, and kept on going.

When we arrived at the Dunes near Muskegon where we were going to camp, I took in the majesty of Lake Michigan. As I started setting up the pup tent, my wife took one look and said asked, "We're both going to sleep in there?" She had never been camping before. This was going to be her first experience. After riding for hours, and pregnant, she would have to sleep on the ground in a little pup tent.

We spent two days there before starting our trip back. The last night we were camping, the group was sitting around the campfire on the shoreline, relaxing and listening to the melodic waves. While no one was paying attention, Jerry picked up a dead fish and slipped the corpse into one of the girls' purses. She didn't find it till the next morning while we were packing to leave. She decided to get even with him. Unknown to any of us, she took that poor fish and slid it into Jerry's sleeping bag on his motorcycle.

The trip back was uneventful, and everybody was tired, but we made it home without incident. Jerry was so tired he just pulled his bike into the garage and didn't remove any gear. The following weekend, he realized he had to go out there and unload that bike. Lo and behold, the rotten fish smell nearly knocked him down when he entered the garage. Jerry couldn't find the aroma's source until he started unloading the bike and discovered the old fish in his sleeping bag. Needless to say, the sleeping bag hit the trash. Quickly. Unfortunately, no photos of our epic Dunes trip survived over the years.

About the same time in 1975, I started another "build-a-bike" project. I had been given a 1969 350 Harley Davidson Sprint. But due to finances and the difficulty in finding the missing parts, I had to sell the Sprint unfinished.

A 1970's era ad for the Harley *Sprint* (Courtesy AMF H-D)

In 1978, after I was laid off from the Dodge main auto plant the second time, Robin and I decided to sell the iconic Honda 350 to a relative.

Our Big Move

After moving to Arizona in the fall of 1979, I was determined to get back on a motorcycle. Happily, I found a 1973 Honda CB 500, with an aftermarket faring, for a whopping $350. The machine had 3200 miles on the odometer. Sadly, the previous owner had laid it down. The Honda was too heavy for him to pick up, and that situation lingered in his mind, so he gave me a great deal. I repaired the dent in the tank, replaced the handlebars, painted the frame, put on tires, and I was back on the road! The lovely four-cylinder Honda was my daily driver for the next six years.

The CB 500

I took the machine camping as often as I could. My favorite motorcycle camping trip occurred when two friends, Mark Blackstone (on his Honda CB 750) and Scott Hall (on his H-D Super Glide), agreed to go along.

On that great trip, our wives rode up on the bikes with us, and we left the kids at home! My brother offered to throw all our gear into his 1966 GTO and follow us up into the forested mountains of Arizona east of Payson (in the area commonly referred to as the Mogollon Rim Country). The ride from the desert floor at 105 degrees transitioned to a beautiful seventy-five degrees at about 7000-foot elevation. We found an old two track road that dropped us down into a small canyon which allowed us to camp right next to Christopher Creek. The road in, and I use that term in the loosest way, was rough. With some special rock placement in the washed-out areas, we were able to make it in on our bikes without mishap. (My brother's GTO picked up a few battle scars on its underside in the process.) The next two days were spent with friends and family enjoying the great outdoors.

The 1966 GTO Goes Camping

Unfortunately, all good things have to pass, and our trip home brought us back to the brutal heat of the desert. When we returned to the Phoenix area, the high for the day was 111 degrees. Let me tell you, it's like standing in front of the oven with your face and body getting cooked by the heat.

I was able to enjoy that bike for years, and I have always appreciated the gratification and memories motorcycle riding has given me.

The Indian *Warrior*
By Doyle Ross

I owned a 1950 Indian Warrior, a 500cc vertical twin motorcycle which had a bad reputation as to longevity. But I loved that little bike and had absolutely no problems with it.

I was drafted into the Army in Oct of 1950, so for the first time in years I was without any kind of motorcycle. After completing basic training, we were allowed to have motor vehicles on base at the Camp Atterbury, Indiana camp. I talked my brother Valta and my friend Glen Witzenburg into hauling the Warrior back to Indiana. My Army life got a whole lot better. A buddy of mine had his Harley there, and he did not think much of my choice of motorcycles. But I made him at least a part believer whenever we hit some nice curvy roads.

The night before the 1951 500-mile auto race in Indianapolis, I was lying on my bunk after lights out, moaning about wanting to go the race and being out of money. Another soldier heard me and said, "If you shut up, I will loan you ten bucks." I got into my civvies, and by ten pm I was on the road up to Indianapolis on my little bike. I knew the road as I had driven past the racetrack a few weeks earlier. When I turned on to W 16 St, I only got a few blocks and I had to stop as the cars were double parked for miles waiting for the gates to open the next morning. I parked and readied myself for a real long night. A policeman on a motorcycle pulled up beside me and asked me if I was going to the race. I said yes, and he told me if he had that motorcycle, he would be a lot closer to the gate than where I was parked. So, I started down the middle of the parked cars and got to within ten cars or so of the entrance. Right across the street was the 16th St Speedway and auto races of all types of cars held an all-night event. So, the night was a whole lot better than I had planned. The next day I realized my childhood dream and got to see and hear the Indy 500.

When I was home from the army over the New Year's holiday in 1951, I proposed to my girlfriend, Pat, and much to my delight and surprise, she said yes. We set the date for September 16 of 1951, which was a Sunday. The Friday night before that weekend, I had the Warrior ready for the trip from Indiana to Nebraska. I made sure the chain was oiled and tightened, tires inflated—you know, the whole routine.

Shortly after 6:00 pm, I was on the road heading west. The Warrior, like most motorcycles, had a "sweet spot," and on this bike it was about 57 MPH. We droned through the night. Remember, this was 1951. Two lanes, no cell phone, no roadside assistance, just a great motorcycle, sparse traffic, and perfect weather. And heading home to marry the cutest girl in town. Oh, and I was now a corporal, so I had just received a pay raise. Life was good. I did get lost in Kansas City, but a friendly policeman got me back on track. I remember I was ready to roll, but he wanted to visit. Bored, I suppose. When I was cruising through Kansas, I was getting that numb feeling and beginning to feel the tiredness sneaking in on me. All at once, a right-angle turn materialized on the two lane!

I went straight ahead into a corn field that had been recently picked. No poles, no trees —just a shallow ditch. The Lord does watch over the careless. I was wide-awake now. The sun was coming up when I was cruising west of Seward, Nebraska on two-lane Highway 34, getting pretty close to the end of the journey. Just as I was rolling cross a two-lane bridge, two cars were approaching, and the trailing car suddenly passed the other one. I hugged the guard rail; they both pulled over and we all escaped. Later on, I realized the sun in the eyes of the drivers was probably the cause of the near disaster.

Anyhow, I arrived home okay. Pat and I got the marriage license, I went to a local motorcycle hill climb and TT race on Saturday afternoon, and the wedding came off without a hitch on Sunday evening. That Warrior was a great bike.

Doyle and Pat with the Indian Warrior in Aurora, Nebraska.

The "Wheelie"
By Jann M. Contento

Most often associated with bicycles and motorcycles, the one-wheel riding stunt has fascinated me ever since I can remember. Maybe it was my Schwinn Sting-Ray bicycle in the 1960s or seeing Evel Knievel in the 1970s that got me hooked. Riding a wheelie was, and remains, a really cool deal.

I'm not sure kids these days are impressed by the wheelie. I certainly don't see many kids riding bicycle wheelies where I live now in Arizona. BMX racing has gained popularity with its many racetracks, course challenges, and such, but BMX appears more like physical, non-motorized motocross. Mountain biking can require "popping a wheelie" from time-to-time, but seems those bikes and riders find little value or satisfaction in "riding" a wheelie for the sake of riding a wheelie. Skate boarders jump ramps, and stunts are sometimes performed by the rider on the board's rear wheels, but that is not the same as "pulling" or "riding" a wheelie.

Street Riding

I've seen, from time to time, daredevil type wheelies from guys on powerful newer sport bikes cranking down the freeways at blistering speed, and superbikers on local highways riding wheelies for better than a block or so at a seemingly deadly rate. Crazy!

I had a 1965 Schwinn String-Ray. I bought the used Schwinn from a friend of my brother's with earned paper route money. Anyway, it had the classic twenty-inch tires, chrome fenders that swooped with a flair at the end, a "banana" seat with the official Schwinn emblem, and a knobby treaded rear tire that I had swapped out for the Schwinn racing "slick." The small pedal sprocket enabled me to apply enough leg force, while pulling up on the signature hi-rise handlebars, to ride for quite a while on the rear wheel alone. Some older kids in the neighborhood took to riding wheelies on ten-speed bikes with those ram-like racing handlebars. One lanky kid who lived in a house behind mine could ride one a block or so on his green ten-speed Schwinn varsity model. Impressive!

Riding a wheelie is different than "popping" a wheelie. When popping a wheelie, the front wheel is lifted off the ground for a short while by either pulling on the handlebars of a bicycle or a quick release of the clutch on a motorbike. Riding the wheelie requires a higher skill set.

Evel Knievel and More

I recall seeing Evel Knievel jump a then indoor world record number of city buses lined up bumper-to-bumper at McCormick Place in Chicago in 1973. I saw him close-up wearing his signature red, white, and blue leather suit, and cape, riding a similarly painted Harley-Davidson XR-750. Really cool. Evel rode some impressively long wheelies while warming up for his record-breaking, no bone-breaking (this time) bus jump. Thrilling and successful!

I've witnessed other risky motorcycle stunts, by local unknowns, and although somewhat entertaining, just didn't match the wheelie. Here a few things I recall as "motorcycle stunts."

Sparks

Some kid from the public high school once fashioned a pair of heavy metal-soled boots in his shop class. He had a Honda CB 750 with the throttle-grip-adjust-screw-cruise-control feature. Late one fall afternoon, when school was letting out and a good crowd of students was lined-up outside waiting on a school bus, this kid mounted his CB 750 wearing his metal-soled boots.

Riding his Honda on the main street fronting the high school, he proceeded to set the cruise control, released both hands from the bars, slid back on the saddle past the passenger strap and, holding on the rear seat grip bar, lowered his metal boots to the asphalt from the passenger foot pegs. As he crouched in a water-skiing position, a fountain of sparks rocketed from the bottom of his boots, creating a collective sparkling stream. All the while, he was being pulled by the driverless CB 750 at 35 miles per hour! He then proceeded to climb back aboard the bike, regained control of the handlebars, and with a satisfied wave, disappeared down the frontage road. Astonishing!

Carnival

A traveling carnival would come to my hometown once a year in the spring. One year, as part of the carnival acts, a large metal shaped globe-like spherical cage was set up with a motorcycle inside. Beside the cage on a small table was what looked like a manually operated grade school free hand clock. Time was set for 7:00 pm with the words "Show Time" written underneath. My best friend and I were there at 5:30 pm, anticipating the caged rider.

At around 6:45, a growing audience began to gather near the globed cage. We had already secured a front and center view a few feet away from the cage. Around 7:15, a tall, hat-wearing man in a vertical-striped shirt introduced the stunt rider as "Fearless Freddy, the Mad Motorcycle Man." Then a trailer door creaked and opened near the back of the roped-off event area.

Outstepped a ruffled old whiskered fella resembling a dusty prospector from earlier times. But he was wearing an open-faced, well-worn grey helmet and wide-cuffed leather riding gloves. He ducked into the small door opening to the cage and climbed aboard the motorcycle. The Tall man hurriedly secured the door latch. Fearless Freddy shook his clenched fisted glove at a balloon attached to the very center top of the cage. Next, the Mad Motorcycle Man single kick-started the bike. A loud four-stroke, with an un-muffled rumble, startled the crowd. Old Freddy was revving the throttle for what seemed like forever before engaging a gear.

Releasing the clutch, the wild stunt man began circumventing the interior of the metal cage. He was blasting around and around at a lower levels, then higher and higher, faster and faster, defying gravity within the small cage. Fearless indeed, Freddy transformed into a noisy blurred object, upside down, head over heels, circling 360 degrees, around and around and around within the caged globe. No one in the now-dizzy crowd had noticed the balloon had popped!

"Fearless Freddy, the Mad Motorcycle Man," had apparently achieved his goal. The machine and the man started their descent, around and around, the noisy bike slowing, heading lower and lower to the floor of the cage. The images, sounds, and smells of that event remain with me today. Star Struck!

Kawasaki 175

In 1973, I owned a Kawasaki 175 Bushwhacker. The torque produced by this high-reving two-stroke allowed me to crank some good wheelies in second gear. I remember changing the stock muffler for a "Hooker" header, providing the cycle more sound and seemingly more horsepower. We mostly performed wheelies on unpaved roads and dirt areas, which minimized potential physical injury from a wheelie mishap. Many of my buddies at the time could ride far more sustained and risky wheelies than I, something I certainly admired. One guy named Bert had a 1971 100cc Hodaka Super Rat. He could ride a wheelie on that Hodaka more than a block at a time, continuously feathering the throttle while sitting comfortably in the saddle. Spectacular!

Motocross

Wheelie riding and such stunts introduced me to motocross racing, or at least to events where I believed I was racing. I had a 1974 Honda Elsinore CR125 with the silver tank and fenders and a green race number panel. Although the Elsinore certainly looked cool, I had to keep from doing wheelies when racing, particularly on hill jumps when contact with the ground helped retain rear tire traction, which was so important in maintaining competitive racetrack times.

XT-500

A few years later, my friend Bert and I both had Yamaha XT-500s. His was a burnt orange 1977 model and mine a silver gray 1978. I never really competed in wheelie riding contests with him or anyone else, for that matter. I was a cautious one-gear wheelie person; pull her up in second gear and ride as long as rpms and balance could keep me there. My pal, known as "The Flying Hawaiian," was fearless. He would begin his wheelie in second and progress through fourth gear with no more than a slight dip in the front wheel's suspended position, reaching a speed above forty miles per hour. Amazing!

I rarely attempt wheelies anymore. I'm kind of hoping my memories of such cool things can keep me floating on a single wheel. Funny the things one thinks about these days.

My Motorcycle Adventures
By Ken Boltz

My adventures in motorcycle riding began at an early age. When I was fifteen years old, a high school friend said, "Let's go to the desert and ride my dirt bikes for an off-road adventure." Of course, I was not about to pass up this opportunity.

We trailered up and drove out to the desert with Yamaha 125cc and 250cc dirt-bike style motorcycles. We began our desert trek in the southwest region of Phoenix near where Phoenix Raceway is now located. Wearing only blue jeans, a white t-shirt, and sneakers, and no real safety riding apparel to speak of, I immediately jumped on his smaller dirt bike and pulled it off the trailer. He grabbed the other. With only minutes of lessons behind us, and having never really ridden, we took off.

I immediately wanted to see how fast I could go and how much fun I could have. Soon as I got on the small Yamaha, I was in heaven. We were riding along a dirt path to get to where the real fun would be. Then, we met our turnoff and rode through some desert. After about a half hour of reckless abandonment riding in somewhat smooth desert terrain, we stopped for a water break, and I had a grin ear-to-ear. Now it was my turn to ride the big, much more powerful motorcycle. So, I hopped on the larger, and superfast, 250cc beast.

When I straddled this mammoth motorcycle, I could not touch the ground with both feet, which should have told me this was a bad idea. But that was not going stop me. I hopped on and took off. WOW! What an exhilarating rush I felt as I started riding. We went through the gears, starting slower and eventually riding faster and faster, jamming through curves and bumps with a joy only an off-road enthusiast would understand.

I was aggressively riding this uncertain terrain. Suddenly, we came up to a curve I wasn't skilled enough, nor prepared enough, to negotiate. At that moment, I realized how under-skilled, and certainly under-dressed, I was for the occasion. I crashed and landed upside down in a cactus tree! Next, I heard someone rushing over to shut off the motorcycle lying on the ground about fifteen feet away. The bike was still roaring away since I had been abruptly separated from it. Riderless, the 250 was screaming. Finally, the noise stopped.

Then, my friend was rushing over to me to see if I had been injured. Suddenly, I saw a hand reaching in to get me. He was leaning in the best he could through the thorns of the cactus to help. After some struggle, a quick few minutes later, I was freed from the spiney tree. However, I was shaking. After realizing I was clear from the brush, I looked myself over closely for injuries, only to find scratches and bruises around my body, along with torn clothing.

I told my friend I was okay to ride and recommended going back slower just in case I was injured from the ordeal. In reality, I said that because I was still jarred from the incident, mostly mentally. I had been riding without proper gear or experience and "outpacing" my actual abilities. Once we arrived back to the vehicle safely, we started to regale the story of my crash, just like kids, laughing and whooping it up.

After this eventful dirt bike ride, I realized I was hooked on the glorious thrill I had received from riding a two-wheeled machine. I had to have my own motorcycle and learn more appropriate riding skills. I also realized I needed to purchase much-needed protective riding gear for safety. The crash itself did not sway my new-found love of motorcycle adventures. My love only grew stronger.

Today, decades later, I have had many motorcycles, both off-road and street. But my lesson from crashing was a critical one. I learned to ride motorcycles within my capabilities, to continue always learning and riding in a better capacity, and to wear and use riding apparel appropriate for the type of motorcycle ride.

I have crashed since; however, sporting correct safety equipment, in particular a helmet, has saved my life.

The silver lining is that I truly am grateful for the crazy kid I was and the day I crashed in the desert. I realized how important motorcycle riding is to me, and I also learned some very valuable lifelong lessons. That day, I found the lifelong passion of riding and my appreciation and love for the sport. I was introduced to the immense joy motorcycling brings me, but I also learned to respect motorcycling and to consider the dangers it presents.

The Zundapp Crash and My Golf Beginnings
By Harry "Happy" Reynolds

In the late fifties, when I was about fourteen and living in Phoenix, Arizona, I had a Zundapp 200cc two-stroke motorcycle. The German-made bike made about twelve HP and required pre-mixing the oil and gas. It had a four-speed gear box and smoked profusely. Because I was fourteen at the time, I could apparently ride it on the street only after my dad and I had a carburetor governor installed that limited the power output to five horsepower. The bike came from Aurora, Nebraska, specifically from SE Ross and Sons, who sold Indians and Zundapps. Doyle Ross, one of the sons, is my brother-in-law (since 1951). They shipped the bike down to Phoenix. Then, we had the governor installed at Baldy Davis MC in Phoenix for a small fee. Being a typical American kid, I took off the governor as soon as I could, and then the bike would scream along about 60 mph. I rode it up to places like Cave Creek and Saguaro Lake, nice twenty-or thirty-mile jaunts. Sometimes my dad, Dr. Ray H. Reynolds, would ride along on his BSA 500cc single.

During Rodeo Days on March 30, 1959, I was traveling northbound on the new Black Canyon Freeway (I-17), following a big utility truck. Suddenly, the truck made an extremely unexpected turn from the right lane into the left lane. Disaster could not be avoided. I hit the left front wheel of the massive truck. As you know, motorcyclists seldom win out in such collisions. This crash caused severe damage to my right foot. My folks were not "happy." I suppose things could have been much

99

worse. The bike wasn't destroyed, but we were both damaged. I wore an old-school plaster cast to stabilize my foot injury. But there is more to this story.

While I was recovering, and certainly not terrorizing the streets of Phoenix on my Zundapp, I happened to play golf at the nine-hole Town and Country Course north of Camelback High School. Sounds crazy now, but I accepted an invite from a friend of mine to go try golf. I "walked" around the course, loping along with a stout two-inch walking peg under the cast, punching big holes in the greens as we ambled across the golf course.

Ironically, that motorcycle crash started my lifelong passion for golfing. I loved golf immediately, cast and all. April in Phoenix on a golf course—priceless!

Oh, I had other motorcycles after that. I had a Sportster for a while, and a beautiful blue and white CL 450 Honda Scrambler in the 1970s. I'm even hoping to take a motorcycle trip next fall, in Arizona, with my nephew Jeff. But from that first trip to Town and Country, golfing has become a huge and wonderful part of my life. I have golfed all over the USA and even played at St. Andrews, Carnoustie, and Royal Troon courses in Scotland. I play golf as often as I can, and I love it. Golf is my passion, the love of my life next to my wife Donna and my family. Quite a story, huh? I guess every cloud really can have a silver lining.

But I sure enjoyed that smoky Zundapp. Great fun.

A late 50s Zundapp 200cc similar to the machine which launched "Happy's" golf career.

Also available at Rogue Phoenix Press

Southwest by Two-Stroke
Riding Yamaha 350s to California
by
Brian Franzen, Mike Newlun and Jeffrey Ross

Our 1973 motorcycle ride took us from Beatrice, Nebraska, to Philmont Scout Ranch in New Mexico, Albuquerque, Phoenix, San Diego, LA, Vacaville, Lake Tahoe, Denver, and then back to Nebraska. We were teenagers, and we had relatives, friends, acquaintances, and girlfriends to see all along the journey. Some nights we camped out, others we stayed in a friend's travel trailer, and some nights we enjoyed regular beds and access to a swimming pool.

Each of us rode a 350cc two-stroke motorcycles on the 3500-mile trip. We had no cell phones, roadside assistance insurance coverage, custom ear plugs, or sound systems.

The early seventies was different than the sixties, but not that much different. The attraction of the open road and the Pacific Ocean was very powerful. None of us were worried about breaking down or the costs of the trip. We had to go see western America. And we did.

An Excerpt

From York, Nebraska, to Phoenix, Arizona-Brian

The first day of the trip, when Jeff and I rode from York down to Beatrice to meet up with Mike, I forgot to take my watch off my wrist. The next day, I had a good sunburn right where the watch rested. No amount of sunscreen could protect my wrist for the rest of the trip. I applied sunscreen liberally thereafter, but the sunburn blistered and never completely healed for three weeks. I would ride for long periods holding onto the mirror support, which provided shade to my sunburned wrist (and tanned my inner arm).

After our first full day of riding from Nebraska into Kansas, we camped at a rest area outside of Dodge City, Kansas, along US 50. No problem. No concerns for our safety or decision. Today, in 2019, we would probably be arrested for camping in such a place. Back then, we just rolled out our bags by a picnic table and spent the night.

The next day, we went past Springfield, Colorado and just before turning south toward Pritchet, Colorado, Mike's bike ran out of gas (due to the extended forks that prevented him from fully utilizing the reserve gas in his fuel tank). Jeff and I kept riding into town before we realized Mike wasn't with us. We turned back and I pushed him into Pritchet by nudging his bike along with my right foot pressed against his left rear shock absorber.

We rode to Philmont Scout Ranch outside Cimarron, New Mexico. (I worked there the previous summer.) We had tent and cot accommodations and got a couple of nice meals and showers because I knew some of the guys at Philmont. I also had an opportunity to visit with some of my old 'colleagues' from the camp.

Then, we headed to Albuquerque. We headed west on Highway 54 from Cimarron to Eagles Nest and on to Red River, NM. We rented little Honda motorcycles and thrashed the mountain roads around Red River. Back on the Yamahas, Team B continued through Taos then down I-25 to Albuquerque where we stayed with my friend Jeanette (who I got to know the previous summer, at Red River, when I worked at Philmont) and her folks. Jeanette and I were good friends, but I never saw her again after we rode out of Albuquerque.

Jeff, Mike, and I slept out in a small travel trailer. Jeanette was into listening to the Johnny Winter *Live* album and Cream. Johnny Winter was playing a live concert in Albuquerque that summer, and his band was a very hot local topic. We took Jeanette and two of her girlfriends on the back of our bikes down I-25 to a mall or someplace after dark. I didn't feel very safe riding on the highway not wearing a helmet (with a face shield) and with a passenger behind me.

Later, well into Arizona, we enjoyed riding down the switchbacks heading into Salt River Canyon, and then ripping back up the canyon curves—a great time on the Yamahas.

You go down about ten miles, curves everywhere, cross the Salt River Bridge at the bottom, then go up through wonderful twisties again for another five or six miles and exit the canyon. Jeff tells me the road has been improved since then, but US 60 through the Salt River Canyon in 1973 was a real blast for bikes! This is where I lost fifth gear. My bike just wouldn't "find the gear" when I shifted into fifth, so I stayed in fourth gear as high gear the rest of the trip.

When we were east of Phoenix, we rolled through Globe, Arizona. Not a pretty town. Globe was a mining town. Rich in history, though. Billy the Kid apparently rustled some cattle around there in 1877 or so. I believe the last stagecoach robbery in American history happened, back in 1899, near Globe, too. I recall the city was hot and dusty as we drove past the big open-pit mine.

Somewhere after Globe, still on Highway 60, during the late afternoon, probably near Superior and the Bluebird Mine area, we were riding through some pitched and curvy section of the highway when a blue VW Beetle (the old-fashioned Beetle) swerved into my lane and nearly took me out. We had been gazing into the sun and moving in and out of patches of shade created by the canyon walls. Good thing I saw that Beetle and avoided a crash. That rattled us a little bit, and we had to pull over and regroup before riding the last forty miles or so into Phoenix.

We made it to Phoenix and enjoyed the hospitality of Jeff's grandparents. They lived near 40th Street and Indian School at the time. We also appreciated their air-conditioning and swimming pool. Just outside the sliding door in the room where we slept was their swimming pool, which was so cool to have so close. We swam a lot, even after dark. I was impressed by the low berms surrounding their entire lot—both front and back yards. The berms were used to contain water used to irrigate their lawn and trees. But other than swimming, we pretty much stayed indoors and rested and avoided the heat.

We did get out to visit a motorcycle shop. As I mentioned, I had lost fifth gear on my motorcycle someplace during the Salt River Canyon run. I would keep up in fourth gear ok, but a higher RPM multiplied the vibration and the engine whine. I got a larger-count counter-shaft sprocket at Apache Cycles in Mesa, Arizona which trimmed the higher RPM a little bit for the rest of the trip. (I didn't want to get the transmission overhauled at this point of the trip—time, work, and money!) This was a clever solution and dropped the rpms to a suitable level at sixty-five mph. I believe this was the only mechanical issue we suffered on the trip, other than Mike's occasional low gas problem. While we were in Mesa, we also visited Jeff's aunt and uncle, Deanna and Steve Cooley.

Albuquerque and more—Jeff

We spent the night in a travel trailer, or maybe it was a camper shell on jacks, in Albuquerque. The trailer was parked, next to Jeanette's house, on a concrete driveway or apron. At some point in the late evening, Team Black Rock was sitting out on lawn chairs just outside the trailer. The three girls were inside the trailer whispering about witches and brujas and ghosts! After things settled down, we could call it a night. No, the trailer was not haunted. Fun.

The ride south from Albuquerque to Socorro and then west to Arizona is interesting. Lots of open high desert, rolling hills, and big skies. I-25 runs near the Rio Grande River and heads south to the city of Socorro. (Why Socorro? "Socorro" means "help" in Spanish. Apparently, a group of worn-out Spanish settlers were given water and food here by local indigents in 1598. The settlement then received its event-marking name: Socorro). At Socorro, motorists can pick up US 60. There are several picturesque New Mexico villages along the way, including

Quasimodo, Pie Town, and Magdalena. At the time, the Very Large Array radio telescope installation was being built about fifty miles west of Socorro. We didn't see any of the large dish radio telescopes back then that dot the landscape today. We just noticed bulldozers, trucks, and surveyors. US 60 West across New Mexico, while scenic and peaceful, is brutal in one respect. A vicious head wind is usually blowing during the spring and summer months.

Arizona has several climate zones: high plateau in the northern third, forest in the middle, and desert in the south. Elevations and scenery change abruptly. Steep mountain grades and brake check turn-outs abound. A totally interesting place, seldom mentioned, is Gonzales Pass, about seven miles west of Superior on US 60.

After rolling along at 2500 feet elevation on a curvy mountain road or so for several miles, you suddenly crest the pass and then can look out across the burning Sonoran Desert toward Phoenix. The flat landscape, and dusty haze, and sporadic desert peaks rising from the desert floor, especially when gazing into the late afternoon summer sun, provide for a stunning vista. And as you descend on a motorcycle, the rise in temperature as you drop 1000 feet or so is very noticeable. Into the furnace!

VISIT OUR WEBSITE
FOR THE FULL INVENTORY
OF QUALITY BOOKS:

http://www.roguephoenixpress.com

Representing Excellence in Publishing

Quality trade paperbacks and downloads
in multiple formats,
in genres ranging from historical to contemporary romance,
mystery and science fiction.
Visit the website then bookmark it.
We add new titles each month!

Made in the USA
Middletown, DE
04 July 2021